SHEPHERD'S NOTES

When you need a guide through the Scriptures

Leviticus/ Numbers

BROADMAN
&HOLMAN
PUBLISHERS

Nashville, Tennessee

Shepherd's Notes®—Leviticus and Numbers
© 1999
by Broadman & Holman Publishers
Nashville, Tennessee
All rights reserved
Printed in the United States of America

0–8054—9069–8
Dewey Decimal Classification: 222:13
Subject Heading: BIBLE. O.T. LEVITICUS
Library of Congress Card Catalog Number: 99–11543

Library of Congress Cataloging-in-Publication Data

House, Paul R., 1958–
    Leviticus & Numbers / Paul House, editor [i.e. author].
        p. cm. — (Shepherd's notes)
    Includes bibliographical references.
    ISBN 0–8054–9069–8 (pbk.)
    1. Bible. O.T. Leviticus—Study and teaching.   2. Bible. O.T. Numbers—Study and teaching   I. Title.   II. Title: Leviticus and Numbers. III. Series
    BS1255.5.H68   1999
    222'.1307—dc21   99–11543
                                                                          CIP

1 2 3 4 5   03 02 01 00 99

CONTENTS

Dear Reader:

Shepherd's Notes are designed to give you a quick, step-by-step overview of every book of the Bible. They are not meant to be substitutes for the biblical text; rather, they are study guides intended to help you explore the wisdom of Scripture in personal or group study and to apply that wisdom successfully in your own life.

Shepherd's Notes guide you through the main themes of each book of the Bible and illuminate fascinating details through appropriate commentary and reference notes. Historical and cultural background information brings the Bible into sharper focus.

Six different icons, used throughout the series, call your attention to historical-cultural information, Old Testament and New Testament references, word pictures, unit summaries, and personal application for everyday life.

Whether you are a novice or a veteran at Bible study, I believe you will find *Shepherd's Notes* a resource that will take you to a new level in your mining and applying the riches of Scripture.

In Him,

David R. Shepherd
Editor-in-Chief

SHEPHERD'S NOTES

HOW TO USE THIS BOOK

DESIGNED FOR THE BUSY USER

Shepherd's Notes for Leviticus and Numbers is designed to provide an easy-to-use tool for getting a quick handle on of these significant Bible books' important features, and for gaining an understanding of their messages. Information available in more difficult-to-use reference works has been incorporated into the *Shepherd's Notes* format. This brings you the benefits of many advanced and expensive works packed into one small volume.

Shepherd's Notes are for laymen, pastors, teachers, small-group leaders and participants, as well as the classroom student. Enrich your personal study or quiet time. Shorten your class or small-group preparation time as you gain valuable insights into the truths of God's Word that you can pass along to your students or group members.

DESIGNED FOR QUICK ACCESS

Bible students with time constraints will especially appreciate the timesaving features built into the *Shepherd's Notes*. All features are intended to aid a quick and concise encounter with the heart of the messages of Leviticus and Numbers.

Concise Commentary. Short sections provide quick "snapshots" of the themes of these books.

Outlined Text. Comprehensive outlines cover the entire text of Leviticus and Numbers. This is a valuable feature for following each book's flow, allowing for a quick, easy way to locate a particular passage.

Shepherd's Notes. These summary statements or capsule thoughts appear at the close of every key section of the narratives. While functioning in part as a quick summary, they also deliver the essence of the message presented in the sections which they cover.

Icons. Various icons in the margin highlight recurring themes in Leviticus and Numbers aiding in selective searching or tracing of those themes.

Questions to Guide Your Study. These thought-provoking questions and discussion starters are designed to encourage interaction with the truth and principles of God's Word.

DESIGNED TO WORK FOR YOU

Personal Study. Using the *Shepherd's Notes* with a passage of Scripture can enlighten your study and take it to a new level. At your fingertips is information that would require searching several volumes to find. In addition, many points of application occur throughout the volume, contributing to personal growth.

Teaching. Outlines frame the text of Leviticus and Numbers, providing a logical presentation of their messages. Capsule thoughts designated as "Shepherd's Notes" provide summary statements for presenting the essence of key points and events. Application icons point out personal application of the messages of the books. Historical Context icons indicate where cultural and historical background information is supplied.

Group Study. *Shepherd's Notes* can be an excellent companion volume to use for gaining a quick but accurate understanding of the messages of Leviticus and Numbers. Each group member can benefit from having his or her own copy. The *Note's* format accommodates the study of themes throughout Leviticus and Numbers. Leaders may use its flexible features to prepare for group sessions or use them during group sessions. Questions to Guide Your Study can spark discussion of key points and truths to be discovered in the books of Leviticus and Numbers.

LIST OF MARGIN ICONS USED IN
LEVITICUS AND NUMBERS

Shepherd's Notes. Placed at the end of each section, a capsule statement provides the reader with the essence of the message of that section.

Historical Context. To indicate historical information—historical, biographical, cultural—and provide insight on the understanding or interpretation of a passage.

Old Testament Reference. Used when the writer refers to Old Testament passages or when Old Testament passages illuminate a text.

New Testament Reference. Used when the writer refers to New Testament passages that are either fulfilled prophecy, an antitype of an Old Testament type, or a New Testament text which in some other way illuminates the passages under discussion.

Personal Application. Used when the text provides a personal or universal application of truth.

Word Picture. Indicates that the meaning of a specific word or phrase is illustrated so as to shed light on it.

INTRODUCTION

Congratulations! Either you are a committed Bible student or you are a courageous person. After all, you are beginning a study of Leviticus and Numbers, two books rarely read by Christians these days. This lack of interest is understandable, yet sad. It is understandable because these books are not easy to read, given our historical distance from them. It is understandable because we rarely hear sermons based upon them. It is understandable because we misunderstand the roles of law and grace in the Bible.

At the same time, it is sad because we cut ourselves off from an exciting and convicting portion of God's Word. Our lack of interest may reveal an alarming laziness among us, since we do not wish to work hard enough to grasp all God has said. In neglecting Leviticus and Numbers, we deprive ourselves of background for the rest of Scripture and of guidance for today.

Frankly, reading Leviticus and Numbers can be an exciting venture for several reasons. First, you may be one of the few believers in your church who has done so. You're a pioneer in the Word! Second, you will gain valuable foundations for biblical history and theology. For example, your appreciation for Christ's death for our sins will be magnified. Third, you will gain life lessons by assessing the actions of the characters in the accounts. There is much we can learn from people like Moses, Aaron, Balaam, and Joshua. There is no doubt, then, that the effort expended in the study of Leviticus and Numbers is well worth it. The message of these books can transform lives.

HISTORICAL SETTING

Leviticus and Numbers were written by Moses during Israel's time in the desert prior to the invasion of the Promised Land (Canaan). There are two possible dates for their journeys. Some scholars think the events occurred about 1450–1400 B.C., while others believe they happened about 1290–1250 B.C. There are good arguments for both positions, and there are Bible-believing experts on both sides of the issue. This book accepts the 1450–1400 B.C. dating, though it recognizes the expertise of those who disagree.

The specific historical setting for Leviticus and Numbers begins in the book of Exodus. Israel had been in Egypt for some four hundred years. During Joseph's era the Israelites had fared well, but by Moses' time the people had become enslaved (Exod. 1:8–14), just as God had warned Abraham in Genesis 15:13 some six centuries earlier. After calling Moses to lead Israel (Exod. 3–4), God intervened by sending ten plagues against Egypt that forced Pharaoh, king of Egypt, to let the people go (Exod. 5–12). He then led the people through the Red Sea, drowning the Egyptian armies in the process (Exod. 13–15).

This deliverance did not unfold during a period of Egyptian weakness. In fact, the years 1500–1200 B.C. found Egypt in a strengthened position brought about by the expulsion of foreign rulers, the renewal of culture, and the pursuing of major building projects. God's victory over this particular Pharaoh, then, demonstrated His great power and His great love for Israel.

In order to prepare the people to possess the Promised Land, the Lord led Israel to avoid immediate warfare by traveling a desert route east (13:17–18). Desert life was not easy. Water was sometimes scarce (15:22–27). God had to supply a miraculous source of food or the people could not have survived (16:1–36). Some battles had to be fought even in the desert (17:8–16). The people complained about these conditions (15:24; 16:2; 17:3), few realizing that God had met their needs before and would do so again. Moses faced many challenges as he led the chosen people! After three months of travel, Israel reached Mount Sinai, where they received the Ten Commandments and God's standards for life and worship (Exod. 19–40). They remained at Mount Sinai for a year before setting out toward Canaan (Num. 1:1).

Thus, Leviticus includes material written in the year between the Exodus and the breaking of camp from Mount Sinai. Numbers, on the other hand, was composed over a thirty-eight-year period during which the Israelites refused to invade Canaan and the first generation subsequently died. The orderly nature of Leviticus and the more hectic nature of Numbers testify to the circumstances in which both were written.

AUTHOR, DATE, AND AUDIENCE

Though scholars have debated the issue for over a century, the biblical text indicates that Leviticus and Numbers were written or dictated to scribes by Moses. Exodus 17:14; 24:4; 34:27, as well as Numbers 33:2 and Deuteronomy 31:9, state that Moses wrote significant portions of these books. It is also true that throughout the Old and New Testaments, the Bible considers the first five books of the Bible (often called the

Law or the Pentateuch) as the work of Moses (Josh. 1:7; 1 Kings 2:3; Neh. 8:1; John 5:45–46). Leviticus claims repeatedly that its contents are the words of God, conveyed to Moses, and committed to writing (1:1; 4:1; 6:1).

God uses all kinds of people, none of whom are sinless. He highlights our strengths, heals our weaknesses, empowers us, and forgives our sins.

Of course, the books are written with Moses described in third person rather than in auto-biographical form. It may be that this was the standard form for writing history in his time, or it may be that one or more of the elders in Numbers 7:1–89 helped Moses write the texts. In the latter case, it would be appropriate for the elders to write in third person under Moses' leadership.

Moses had a special relationship to God. He spoke directly with the Lord (Exod. 33:7–11), was given the Law by God, and received direct revelation from the Lord. Moses was a volatile man, one who had killed in the past (Exod. 2:11–14), and one whose rash action cost him the chance to go to the Promised Land (Num. 20:1–12). At the same time, he was a humble man, one dedicated to the Lord with his whole heart (Num. 12:3). His leadership of the people was competent, caring, decisive, and God-centered. His writing is clear, theologically rich, and practical. Written under the inspiration of the Holy Spirit, these books have inspired and instructed people of faith for over three thousand years.

Here *inspiration* means that God spoke to the author (Moses) directly. God also took Moses' personality into account when leading him to write, for the Pentateuch does not sound just like other books of the Bible. Thus, God used Moses to write, yet gladly used Moses' human gifts.

The events described in Leviticus and Numbers unfolded during 1450–1400 B.C., and they were written during this era as well. As part of the Law, they are in the oldest part of the Bible accepted as Scripture by the believing community. The prophetic and poetic books cite materials from these books, as do some New Testament passages.

The original audiences for Leviticus and Numbers were not the same. Leviticus was written during the first year of Israel's desert sojourn to the first generation to leave Egypt. This group was comprised mainly of Abraham's descendants, though representatives from other ethnic heritages were represented as well (Exod. 12:38). One of the more prominent non-Israelites was Caleb, who came to be a significant man of faith in the accounts (cp. Num. 13–14). God's love was not then—nor is it now—restricted to a single ethnic group. Faith was then and is now the criterion for being part of the people of God, and Caleb had that faith. The purpose of Leviticus was to instruct Israel in the way they were to live. God intended them to be a holy people and a kingdom of priests (Exod. 19:5–6; Lev. 11:44), and He wanted them to live in a rich, loving, and generous society that proclaimed His glorious nature. To this end God gave them the words of Leviticus.

Numbers, on the other hand, was directed to the second generation of Israelites, the one that eventually conquered the Promised Land. This group learned from their parents' mistakes. They determined to follow the Lord and keep His commands, and they were rewarded with an impressive string of triumphs. Though the audience is different, the main intent of Numbers is the same as that of Leviticus: to instruct Israel in how to be a holy nation that will declare the Lord's great worth. This purpose is achieved by the revealing of God's commands and by recounting events that warn and encourage the readers.

According to Hebrews 11:1, "Faith is the assurance of things hoped for, the conviction of things not seen" (NASB). The object of faith is God, and the content of faith is found in the Scriptures.

The names *Leviticus* and *Numbers* originate from Latin words. The Hebrew names for the books are: "And God Called" (Leviticus) and "In the Desert" (Numbers), which are more descriptive of the books' contents and theology.

THE CONTENTS OF THE BOOKS

Though some of the books' materials are hard to understand because of our distance from their origins, the texts unfold in a rather straightforward manner. To grasp the structure of Leviticus, it is necessary to note how Exodus concludes. First, Exodus 19–24 states God's initial giving of commands and case laws. These standards are from God and are thus fair and right and good. Second, Exodus 25–31 orders the building of a portable sanctuary for Israel's use while in the desert. Third, Exodus 32–34 describes the golden calf incident, where Israel made an idol a scant few weeks after receiving the Ten Commandments. Moses interceded and God forgave the nation. Fourth, Exodus 35–40 depicts the actual construction of the worship center specified in Exodus 25–31. When Exodus ends, the people have a place to worship and standards for judging the difference between good and evil behavior.

The Levites were a tribe (clan) of Israel. Levi was one of Jacob's twelve sons. His descendants were singled out as the ones to focus on priestly tasks.

With these notions in place, Leviticus 1–7 explains sacrifices for sin that may be offered at the worship center. Next, Leviticus 8–10 sets apart the Levites as the ones who will lead worship at the worship site where the sacrifices will be made. Then, Leviticus 11–16 discusses situations and conditions that make a person unable, inappropriate, or excused from normal community life. Such persons are relieved of the responsibility of participating in worship or barred from doing so, depending on their situation. Finally, Leviticus 17–27 states how the people may live holy lives for the Lord. Such living would mean that sacrifices of praise will be offered much more often than sacrifices for sin. Leviticus intends to create a holy society in which sins are confessed and forgiven, in which debts are canceled, in which rape and abuse are absent, and in which neighbors love one another as they love themselves.

Numbers begins where Leviticus ends. The nation now has a place to worship, in which they will be led by choice leaders who will help them make sacrifices and become increasingly more faithful in their walk with God. Therefore, it seems that the nation is now ready to conquer the Promised Land. So Numbers 1:1–10:10 recounts their moving from Mount Sinai to the border of Canaan, the Promised Land. Numbers 10:11–20:21 describes the people's journey from the borders of Canaan to the desert called Kadesh Barnea. What has happened? Why are they not in Canaan? Because of rebellion born of unbelief. Numbers 20:22–36:13 ends the book by taking the nation from Kadesh Barnea back to the edge of the Promised Land. The first generation has passed from the scene, and the new, faithful generation has taken its place. Ultimate victory will come soon.

Theology comes from Greek and means "the study of God." Every person has a theology, for every person has an idea of what he or she thinks about God. Christians must strive to know and practice what the Bible teaches about God.

THE THEOLOGY OF LEVITICUS AND NUMBERS

The outlines of Leviticus and Numbers reveal the books' main theological emphases. The four parts of Leviticus are tied together by the story of Israel, as well as by distinctive words and phrases. Leviticus 1–7 emphasizes the offering of sacrifices for sins. In this way it describes the God who forgives. In Leviticus 8–10 the Lord separates the sanctuary and the Levites as special to Him. God calls and equips His servants. Leviticus 11–16 emphasizes how people may be ready to enter the Lord's sanctuary. Thus, here the Lord is portrayed as the God who explains appropriate habits and lifestyles to Israel. Forgiveness remains an important theme here as

Holiness literally means "separate," or "set apart." It also means "personal purity as one fulfills one's set apart purpose." God's holiness is total, while people are dependent on God for their holiness. A holy person or thing is set aside for God's purposes. Holy persons do God's will.

God's presence through the Holy Spirit is guaranteed to all believers (Eph. 1:13–14). Because God is with us, we need not fear life's great trials (Rom. 8:28–39). God's presence also means that we can be sure that our salvation is secure in Christ (John 10:28–29).

well. Finally, Leviticus 17–27 offers extensive regulations for those wanting to be holy for the Lord. Throughout this section, the text emphasizes that God is holy and therefore commands Israel to be holy.

God's holiness permeates the book. From the holy sanctuary and its holy implements, to the holiness of obedient behavior, to the holiness of God's character, the idea never leaves Leviticus. Related to holiness is the notion that the Lord is present among His people. The ceremonies in Leviticus are designed to foster communion between God and Israel. This fellowship is based upon how well Israel's commitment to holiness matches God's holiness.

Numbers connects with Leviticus both historically and theologically. Having received the standards in Leviticus, the people prepare to leave Mount Sinai in Numbers 1:1–10:10. This passage declares that the Lord guides and inspires Israel. Numbers 10:11–20:21 describes Israel's constant rebellion against God. Despite their sinfulness, the Lord shows Himself to be the one who provides for Israel. Numbers 20:22–36:13 finds Israel once again headed toward the Promised Land, which indicates that God renews promises to faithful persons.

Taken together, the books of Leviticus and Numbers claim that God forgives, calls ministers, instructs, is holy, guides and inspires, protects and provides, and renews promises. In other words, they state that God is faithful. God never falters or fails or lies. God can be counted upon in every life setting. The question that we must ask is whether we are faithful. We must decide to make this theology more relevant to our daily lives than so many of the Israelites did in their time.

LEVITICUS AND NUMBERS IN THE REST OF THE BIBLE

Leviticus and Numbers are not cited in the rest of the Bible as often as books like Isaiah and Psalms, but their influence is apparent nonetheless. For instance, several Old Testament texts reflect the importance of the sacrifices that Leviticus introduces. Isaiah 1:10–17, Jeremiah 7:21–26, and Malachi 1:6–9 all complain that the people bring sacrifices, but that they do not bring them with sincere and repentant hearts. Sacrifices offered without faith and humility are not sacrifices that God honors. Psalm 51:16–19 also testifies to the need for a contrite and broken heart when a person brings sin offerings.

The Old Testament stands steadfastly against legalism, which is the belief that the mere completion of religious duties please God. Faith must be the reason for worship and obedience. Works alone cannot satisfy the Lord. They are significant as they are generated by faith.

Isaiah 52:13–53:12 provides an important link between the Old Testament sacrifices and the New Testament's claim that Jesus' death removes sin. Isaiah 53:10 calls the person who dies for the people a "guilt offering," the only time the Old Testament speaks favorably of a human sacrifice.

In the New Testament, several passages identify Jesus as this guilt offering (John 12:38; Rom. 10:16; Matt. 8:17; 1 Pet. 2:22, 24–25; Luke 22:37). These inspired writers believe that Jesus is the one whose death can remove the sins of those who put their trust in Him.

Of course, the book of Hebrews comments on the sacrificial system more than any other New Testament book. The heart of the message of Hebrews is not that the Old Testament sacrifices were bad, but that Jesus' death is even greater than those God-given ones. As Hebrews 10:1–18 indicates, Jesus' death was a final, non-repeatable, and sufficient sacrifice. This makes it superior to the perpetual nature of the offerings of Leviticus.

Christ removes sin once and for all. Until the time of Christ, animal sacrifices were acceptable. Now, however, the work of Christ renders the Old Testament sacrifices ineffective. They are obsolete only by divine decree and divine self-sacrifice (Heb. 10:12–18). Though absolutely essential until Christ's death, the old system no longer applies to people of faith. Despite these facts, it is important to understand that without a grasp of the old system one cannot know what Christ has done for us.

Numbers is used in the rest of the Bible in three basic ways. First, the rebellion accounts are cited elsewhere to explain why the Lord punished Israel (Deut. 1:26–40; Ezek. 20:13–16; Ps. 78:17–19, 40–55). Second, the rebellions are mentioned to emphasize ingratitude in light of God's marvelous, kind, merciful provision for their needs (Jer. 2:6, 3:12–14; Ezek. 20:17; Pss. 78:38; 136:16). Such kindness should have bound them to the Lord forever, but such was not their response. Third, Psalm 95:7–11, which is quoted in Hebrews 3:15–4:7, counsels readers not to harden their hearts as the Israelites did. Similarly, the apostle Paul warns the Corinthians to avoid the mistakes the Israelites made in the desert. He does so to teach them how to withstand temptation, and to help them read the Old Testament as a book of positive and negative examples for their Christian lives (1 Cor. 10:1–13).

LEVITICUS AND NUMBERS IN TODAY'S WORLD

We should read Leviticus and Numbers the way the Bible itself interpreted them. Leviticus can help us know how to live holy lives and how to confess and find forgiveness for our sins. Numbers should stand as warnings and encouragements for us to do the Lord's will. Reading these texts in this manner will strengthen our

"But this man, after he had offered one sacrifice for sins for ever, sat down on the right hand of God; From henceforth expecting till his enemies be made his footstool. For by one offering he hath perfected for ever them that are sanctified" (Heb. 10:12–14, KJV).

In general, all Old Testament teachings remain valid for today unless the New Testament explicitly sets one aside (see Mark 7:19), or the work of Christ specifically replaces one (see Heb. 10:11–18), or the ability or right to carry out a specific punishment is no longer available (see Rom. 13:1–7). We must be careful to avoid thinking that Jesus set aside every Old Testament law, for He claimed to do the opposite (see Matt. 5:16–20).

Christian walk by teaching us accounts largely forgotten in today's churches.

It is also true that neglecting these books will lead to serious gaps in our theology and ethics. After all, it is in Leviticus that standards against child abuse, bestiality, rape, and homosexuality are covered. Without these references there would be precious little about these and other moral issues in Scripture. Thus, neglecting these books will have a negative effect on the church and society. Obeying them, on the other hand, will strengthen and guide the church in the midst of an increasingly secular culture.

QUESTIONS TO GUIDE YOUR STUDY

1. What were the settings in which Leviticus and Numbers were written?
2. What were the original audiences for Leviticus and Numbers?
3. What attribute of God permeates Leviticus?
4. What are some of the consequences of neglecting Leviticus and Numbers in our own time?

Few portions of Scripture baffle readers more than this one. We are unfamiliar with its rituals, so all we may get from these chapters is a vague sense of horror over the death of innocent animals. It may bother some that the Lord required such sacrifices, or may even cause them to wonder if God *did* command them. We must remember, though, that these sacrifices were not strange to the original audience. To them they were logical, even simple, given their historical context. What was unusual was the fact that they were directed toward one God.

A sacrifice was an "offering" of an animal or cereal that was given in place of one's sins or out of gratitude for God's blessings. Thus, "sacrifice" and "offering" are interchangeable words.

Leviticus 1–7 can be divided into three clear parts:

SCRIPTURE	SUBJECT
Leviticus 1–3	Burnt, grain, and fellowship offerings
Leviticus 4–5	Guilt offerings
Leviticus 6–7	How priests are to receive and officiate over these sacrifices

Each type of sacrifice has its own purpose, but each one emphasizes the seriousness of sin. The death of the animal showed in a graphic way the consequences sin has. The attentive worshiper realized that this animal was taking the consequences of his sin. These sacrifices were substitutionary. The worshiper deserved what was happening to the animal. But in His mercy, God decreed that the worshiper be saved from the penalty of his sin and that the animal bear the penalty. Again, the perceptive worshiper would see enacted in graphic fashion the mercy of God to him. Those who truly worshiped went away from the sacrifice with a heart thankful to God for His grace.

THE BURNT OFFERING (LEV. 1:1–17)

Burnt offerings were most likely the oldest type of sacrifices known to the ancient world. Virtually every major religion offered some type of them, though not for the same reason. Stated simply, a burnt offering was just that—a sacrifice that was totally consumed by fire. The worshiper held nothing back, and the priest received no part of the sacrifice. It all belonged to the Lord.

Like all other sacrifices, the burnt offering was given in place of a sinner's transgressions. What is not altogether clear is what sort of sins were covered by burnt offerings. Apparently burnt offerings were a confession of general sinfulness, not unlike the "forgive us our debts" of the Lord's prayer (see Matt. 6:9–13). Thus, the burnt offering expressed the sinner's total dependence on God for forgiveness. It also pledged the worshiper's commitment to serve the Lord in the future.

Burnt offerings were to be brought to the sanctuary by every Israelite family. Obviously, not every family had the same financial resources. Therefore, different sacrifices were ordered for the rich and the poor. Both were to give appropriately; neither was to be bankrupted in the giving. Those who could afford to do so were to bring a male from their herd or flock (1:10–13); the poor were to bring two birds (1:14–17).

Sacrifices were substitutionary in that they took the place of sin and its penalty. Christ's death for us is therefore substitutionary because it takes the place of our sin and removes the penalty for our sin.

"If we confess our sins, he is faithful and just to forgive us our sins, and to cleanse us from all unrighteousness. If we say that we have not sinned, we make him a liar, and his word is not in us" (1 John 1:9–10, KJV).

13

Priests were to teach the people how to know and approach God. People could pray without them, of course, so they were not the only means by which Israel could come before God. Like today's pastors, they were to make certain that each generation was taught the essential truths of God's Word and help that Word be applied to daily life.

Priests were to serve as helpers and instructors, not as divine power brokers or magicians (1:3–9). They were to tell the people what God had taught Moses. In this way they mediated God's presence for the Israelites. They led people to encounter the Lord in the manner the Lord prescribed, so they helped them to avoid divine anger and secure forgiveness at the same time.

It is important to note how the people gave their sacrifices. The worshiper was to place a hand on the head of the animal (1:4), slaughter the animal (1:5), and then allow the priests to do their work. Placing a hand on the animal emphasized the personal and substitutionary nature of the sacrifice. The act also amounted to a confession of sin.

Thus, the act of worship that dealt with sin was straightforward. A sinner must admit the sin; a sinner must acknowledge that this sin will cost the animal its life; a sinner must accept the financial loss the death of a valuable animal brings. But afterwards a sinner can also enjoy the forgiveness that comes from this process.

THE GRAIN AND FELLOWSHIP OFFERINGS (2:1–3:17)

Like the burnt offering, the grain and fellowship offerings were brought voluntarily by individuals who desired to please God (2:2; 3:5). The chief difference between these sacrifices and the burnt offering was that part of the grain (2:3) and a portion of the fellowship offering meat could be eaten by the priests (see 7:28–36). Clearly, these sacrifices highlighted the communal nature of Israel's worship. Priests and worshipers could enjoy together the blessings of forgiveness and renewed communion with God.

Grain offerings were brought voluntarily to the priests, who proceeded to burn most of them (2:1–2). The rest of the offerings were shared with the priests (2:3). This offering could be given at anytime, but it was especially appropriate at harvest (2:14–16). Its purpose was to recognize God's goodness in providing for the people, and to be generous to God's servants, the priests.

The word for fellowship is *shalom*, which implies wholeness, sound relations, and the absence of conflict. It can also include reconciliation between separated parties.

Fellowship offerings were also voluntary sacrifices that had a community aspect. The word translated *fellowship* literally means "peace," which indicates that this sacrifice was intended to acknowledge that one either needed to be or was at peace with the Lord. Most of the sacrifice was to be consumed by fire (3:1–17), but Leviticus 7:11–21 states that the priests and worshipers could eat the remnant of the sacrifice. In this way, one's joy over being forgiven could be shared with a group of people.

These first three sacrifices set the stage for those that follow. The burnt offering was intended to cover general sins confessed by an honest person. The grain offering expressed appreciation for God's provision and a willingness to share what God had given. Fellowship offerings demonstrated the worshiper's desire to be at peace with God. Forgiveness, gratitude, generosity, and a longing for peace with God, not legalistic obligation, were at the heart of the sacrificial system.

THE SIN OFFERING (4:1–5:13)

So far the text has discussed offerings that address general sin and general joy and gratitude. Now the book begins to cover sacrifices

15

One's status in the church does not remove the responsibility to confess sins. No individual, whether pastor or layperson, fails to sin, so each person must humbly seek God's forgiveness.

Guilt means actual responsibility for the negative effects of sin. It is not just a psychological feeling. It is a real result of a real fault, and it is defined by God's Word.

that relate to specific sins. It does so by explaining situations that might cause a person to need to bring either a sin or a guilt offering. Principles established in chapters 1–3 help readers understand these new sacrifices.

Simply stated, a sin offering was a sacrifice offered for specific unintentional sin. It was required from anyone who sinned, whether that person was a leader, a priest, or a typical citizen. It was also appropriate when the whole community sinned unintentionally. Therefore, these verses do not just introduce a sacrifice, they help define sin as the breaking of God's law by either an individual or a community.

SIN OFFERINGS FOR PRIESTS (4:1–12)

Priests were not above the Lord's law. Indeed, because of their familiarity with God's truth they were more accountable for their actions than an average person. They were to use their privileged position for promoting holiness, not for doing whatever they pleased.

A sin offering was to be brought when the priest sinned unintentionally (4:1). Despite being unintentional, such sins brought guilt on the nation (4:3). Sin has a negative effect even when the sinner does not commit the act flagrantly. The proper offering is a young bull without defect (4:3), which indicated that the substitute for sin was whole and costly.

As with the burnt offering, the sinner placed his hand on the animal's head, thus confessing the offense (4:4). Once the sacrifice was slaughtered, the officiating priest took some of the blood to the altar to the Lord (4:4–7). The animal was then burned and removed from the camp (4:8–12), and its removal from the camp symbolized the removal of sin from the priest and the people.

SIN OFFERINGS FOR THE COMMUNITY (4:13–21)

As was stated earlier, sin is not just an individual matter. What a person does affects others. It is also true that at times whole groups of people can agree together to do the wrong thing. An entire nation, race, community, or family can band together to harm others in some manner. Sin offerings were one way Israel could deal with guilt incurred in this way.

"Wherefore, as by one man sin entered into the world, and death by sin; and so death passed upon all men, for that all have sinned" (Rom. 5:12, KJV).

Verse 13 reminds readers that sin has consequences even when the community is unaware of wrongdoing. Guilt is established by the breaking of God's commandments. Once made aware of their sin, the community was to offer a sacrifice similar to the one the priests gave for their sins (4:14). As the people's representatives, the community elders were charged with the duty of laying confessing hands on the animal (4:15). The priests were then to do as they had done for the sin offering that they themselves had offered (4:16–21). God was just as willing to forgive community sins as individual transgressions of the divine commands.

SIN OFFERINGS FOR LEADERS (4:22–26)

Elders are as accountable to God as the priests and the community. They, too, were responsible for admitting their sin, bringing a proper sin offering, and having the priest take the blood of their substitute before the Lord. Once again, this activity brought pardon for sin and release from its guilt. Why? Because the merciful and gracious God said so.

Forgiveness is a decision made and declared by God. It is not a feeling that we possess. Whenever we confess our sins, the Lord forgives them (1 John 1:9–10), even though we may not feel that this is true. Accepting forgiveness requires faith and trust in the Lord.

SIN OFFERINGS FOR COMMUNITY MEMBERS (4:27–35)

As could be expected by now, the unintentional sins of individual Israelites were not beyond God's grace either. They could also bring an appropriate sin offering and receive the priests' assistance before the Lord. When they did so their sin was "atoned for" (4:31, 35), a phrase that means "covered," which is another way of saying "forgiven" (4:31, 35). These sacrifices had to be repeated, which makes them inferior to Christ's permanent sacrifice for sin (see Heb. 9:11–28). Still, it is vital to understand that the Lord actually forgave those who obeyed His commands about their sins.

Use the Bible to set your mind against sin. Do not just use the Scriptures to know what you did wrong after the fact. This approach will keep us from being unaware of Satan's schemes (see 2 Cor. 2:11).

OCCASIONS THAT REQUIRE SIN OFFERINGS (5:1–13)

Leviticus is not just a manual for defining and offering sacrifices. It spends a great deal of space explaining what actions are sinful and how those actions may be avoided. The book provides readers insights to grasp the nature and effects of sin before someone sins. In this way readers can avoid sin, and thereby learn how to walk with the Lord.

Four situations that necessitated a sin offering are listed here. First, one could sin by not speaking up in a case requiring one's testimony (5:1). Second, one could touch an item, such as a dead animal (5:2), that could make one unclean. (The meaning of the word *unclean* will be discussed in some detail later.) Third, one could touch some human uncleanness (5:3). Fourth, one could take an oath thoughtlessly (5:4). Each of these possibilities could harm the community, either by allowing injustice to prevail or words to become meaningless, or by posing a health risk. Such actions may be unintentional, but they remain harmful nonetheless. Happily, they were forgivable by the same God who declared them wrong. Pardon was secured by the same means as for the offenses committed by the elders, priests, and whole community (5:5–13).

THE GUILT OFFERING (5:14–6:7)

Guilt offerings were the same as sin offerings in all but one respect. Like a sin offering, a guilt offering was given for unintentional sins, but for sins that required restitution. Some sins are against someone or something in general, yet cause no specific financial or personal harm. Others, however, are of such a nature that they cost the harmed party. In such cases there needs to be payment for what has been lost. For Israel, the guilt offering was the proper way to handle sins that had specific costs associated with them.

Three situations are noted that led to guilt offerings. First, a person might sin in some unspecified way against the sanctuary (5:14–16). Second, one could break commands God had explicitly stated (5:17–19). Third, an individual could lie, steal, cheat, or otherwise mistreat a neighbor (6:1–7). In each case a sacrifice akin to a sin offering was to be brought, and a 20 percent fine added to it. The extra money was given to the wronged party. This payment served as a deterrent to repeating the offensive behavior. It also forced the sinner to help create a positive end to the negative thing that had been done.

THE PRIESTS' ROLE IN THE OFFERINGS (6:8–7:38)

To this point the book has focused upon the worshiper's responsibility in the bringing of sacrifices. Now the text moves to the priests' responsibilities and privileges in the forgiveness

These rituals emphasize the seriousness and reverence that ought to characterize worship. Today's churches often seem friendly, yet fail to instill a sense of God's holiness, our sinfulness, God's grace, the necessity of learning God's Word, and the importance of praying for others.

rituals. Every one of the specific sacrifices required the priest to teach and guide the worshiper. Some of the sacrifices could sustain the priest and his family. A few of the offerings carried special instructions, and all the rituals were vital for the people's relationship with God.

Burnt offerings (6:8–13) were to burn continuously. The idea was for the people to stay focused on confession and forgiveness. Israel needed to be humble before the Lord, upon whom they were totally dependent for cleansing and renewal. Priests were to wear specific garments when handling the remains of the offerings, which indicated that the Lord's sacrifices were important—not to be taken lightly.

Grain offerings (6:14–23) were partly consumed and partly shared by the priests (6:15–16). Thus, the priests were sustained by the people's offerings. Only the priests could eat this offering, for the sacrifice was holy, or set apart, for the Lord. Grain offerings given by priests were burned completely (6:19–23). No one else could eat the food or the Lord's offerings would be defiled. Once again the idea was to show how important the sacrifices were to Israel. A failure to take their responsibilities seriously could lead to a fatal continuation in sin.

Sin offerings (6:24–30) could be eaten by the priests (6:29). An exception to this rule was for special sin offerings that were brought into the holy place (6:30). As with the burnt and grain offerings, the people had to learn the sacred nature of the substitute for sin. It was also vital for the priests themselves to understand the holiness of the sacrifices, since they could have been tempted to eat the animals whenever they wished. This problem certainly plagued Israel during Samuel's time (see 1 Sam. 2:12–26).

Guilt offerings (7:1–10) were handled much like sin offerings (7:7). As with the sin offering, part of the guilt offering could be eaten by the priests and their families. It is interesting that the hide of the animals belonged to the priests who administered the sacrifice, perhaps so he could earn a living through tanning or craftsmanship.

> It is appropriate for congregations to show love and appreciation for their ministers. It is not the congregation's responsibility to keep the church staff humble and poor. It is their job to love and honor those who help them know the Lord.

Fellowship offerings (7:11–21) were to be shared and eaten. This sacrifice was a positive expression of a worshiper's love for the Lord and appreciation for the priests. Even such a positive and open offering had to be handled with care, however, or the people could forget its high purpose (7:19–21). Once again it was the priests' responsibility to see that the sacrifice was used properly.

God also instructed the priests to tell the people never to eat the fat or blood of animals (7:22–26). Fat could be used for other purposes, but was not to be eaten (7:24). Explanations of blood's importance come later. Here God simply forbids His people to drink it.

Leviticus 7:28–38 summarizes the teachings of 6:8–7:21. The passage reminds readers of the priests' rights and responsibilities in the offering of sacrifices. It is important to understand that they taught, helped, and received part of their daily sustenance from the sacrifices brought by the Israelites. If the Israelites were unfaithful in bringing their offerings, then the priests would suffer. If the priests were derelict in their duty, then the people would not have a right relationship with the Lord. Each was dependent on the other, a situation that made true community and meaningful fellowship possible.

21

■ *God is holy. He desires that His people be*
■ *holy. God gave Israel various sacrifices to*
■ *picture the consequences of sin and God's*
■ *intention to separate His people from the*
■ *impurities of sin. Five types of sacrifices are*
■ *to be offered. Three deal with sins that have*
■ *been committed while two allow worshipers*
■ *to express joy and gratitude to God.*

QUESTIONS TO GUIDE YOUR STUDY

1. What was distinctive about a burnt offering?
2. How did grain offerings differ from burnt offerings?
3. How were guilt and sin offerings similar? How were they different?
4. What was a fellowship offering?

Moses continues to return to the divine agenda set forth in Exodus 25–31 that was interrupted by the golden calf incident of Exodus 32–34. Exodus 35–40 refocused Israel's attention on building a sacred, holy place where God's presence was to be enjoyed. Leviticus 1–7 explains the sacrifices the Lord accepts in place of human sin. Now Moses gives further directions for priests. These instructions state that God's ministers must be holy so they can serve a holy people (8:1–36), must serve as the holy God directs (9:1–24), and can expect God's judgment when these commands are not obeyed (10:1–20).

SETTING THE PRIESTS APART (8:1–36)

God explained the ceremony found here in Exodus 29. There the Lord states explicitly that these rituals were to "make holy," "set apart," or "consecrate." Aaron and his family were the chosen priests for the chosen people (Exod. 29:1). The ceremony for setting Aaron's family apart was to be done before the congregation (8:1–4). They were to commit themselves to the ministry that the priests would conduct.

"And thus shalt thou do unto Aaron, and to his sons, according to all things which I have commanded thee:seven days shalt thou consecrate them" (Exod. 29:35, KJV).

The service unfolded in seven parts. First, having declared the importance of Aaron's family, Moses placed the priestly garments on Aaron (8:5–9; see Exod. 28:6–43). These clothes were to set Aaron apart from the people. He was not better than they, but his role was different.

Second, Moses anointed Aaron with oil, a process that symbolized God's presence in Aaron's

God's "call" means that He has a specific purpose for an individual's life. God gifts every Christian for service (see 1 Cor. 12), yet also specifically leads some persons to be paid leaders. Each Christian should be open to discovering his or her gifts and calling and serving the Lord appropriately.

life (8:10–13). Aaron was God's choice for this ministry. Because he was God's choice, it was impossible for him to carry out his ministry merely in his own strength. This part of the ceremony also emphasized Aaron's divine calling to the congregation.

Third, Moses helped the new priests offer sacrifices for their sins and celebrate their call to ministry (8:14–29). To this end, they brought sin, burnt, and commemorative offerings. Each symbolized their need for forgiveness even as they aided the people in receiving pardon. They were not above the divine law. They had to identify with the congregation at the same time they prepared to exercise leadership among them.

Fourth, Moses sprinkled blood from the sacrifices on Aaron to set apart his garments (8:30). Fifth, Aaron and his sons ate part of the offering, according to the standards of 6:8–7:38. Everything God commanded was done. Now the nation had a special priesthood to meet their special worship needs. All these rituals were done to make certain that God's grace would be communicated to the people.

SERVING AS GOD COMMANDED (9:1–24)

Leviticus 9 displays the joy and wonder of ministry. Here the priests began to lead the worship God commanded. Here they did so perfectly (9:1–22). Their fidelity to God's Word led to the Lord's approval, which in this instance was demonstrated by God's glory encountering the Israelites. In Exodus 40:34–35 the Lord showed approval of the tabernacle's completion by filling the worship center with glory in the form of a cloud. Now fire came from God's presence and consumed the sacrifices (9:23–24). Israel rejoiced at God's pleasure with them. One could hope that worship could always go this well, though Exodus 32–34 has already shown that not even worship is perfect in a sinful world.

SUFFERING FOR PRESUMPTION (10:1–20)

Gladness turned to sorrow. Once more fire appeared, but this time to punish, not approve. Two of Aaron's sons, Nadab and Abihu, used "alien" or "unauthorized" fire on the altar. It was unauthorized in that it was fire the Lord had not commanded them to use (10:1). Because of their presumption, the Lord sent fire that consumed the men (10:2). This disaster occurred because the priests committed the root sin of the human race: they disobeyed God's Word. They failed in their main job, which was to make the Lord holy in the people's eyes (10:3). Therefore, the Lord showed Himself holy by removing them. These deaths demonstrate the gravity of the priests' service before the Lord. Subsequent events reinforced this point. Moses made it plain that the priests' appearance (10:4–7), sobriety (10:8–9), and eating of the sacrifices (10:12–15) had to be carefully and properly done. Otherwise the people might get the idea that worship is not all that important, which would have led to a lack of proper relationship with God.

Why must the priests be so scrupulous in their observance of God's directions (see 10:16–20)? Why was Yahweh so concerned about the preservation of His holy commands? Two reasons are given. First, 10:10–11 highlights the priests' role as teachers of God's revealed Word. They were not mere religious professionals. They were human bridges to God's truth. Moses

Glory means "heaviness," or the "heaviness of one's presence." Thus, God's glory is His awe-inspiring presence in a place or in one's heart and mind.

Being careful and respectful in worship is not the same thing as joyless legalism. We only enjoy that which we take seriously, and we only take seriously things we consider very important. True joy comes from loving respect for God that results in an enriching relationship, not a dreaded obligation.

shared God's truth with them, and they were to teach Israel what they knew.

Second, through their teaching and ministering the priests helped facilitate forgiveness (10:17). This role's function can hardly be overstated. People looked to them to know how to be right with God. A priest's seriousness about his task, then, was to approximate the Lord's seriousness about sin. Their task was joyous, yet only when taken with the utmost seriousness.

■ *The Lord instituted a priesthood to carry out*
■ *the sacrifices and offerings prescribed. The*
■ *Lord instructed Moses to ordain the priests*
■ *and help them begin their work. The ordina-*
■ *tion ceremony lasted seven days. Aaron's sons*
■ *offered sacrifices in a manner contrary to*
■ *God's command. The entire community wit-*
■ *nessed the consequences of failure to obey God.*

QUESTIONS TO GUIDE YOUR STUDY

1. What were the seven parts of the service in which the priest was set apart?
2. What was the significance of each part of this service?
3. Why were priests to be so careful in the way they observed God's directions?
4. What does the author mean when he says that the tasks of the priests were "joyous, yet only when taken with the utmost seriousness"?

PART THREE THE GOD WHO EXPLAINS APPROPRIATE BEHAVIOR: LEVITICUS 11–16

The laws found in these chapters are particularly hard for readers to understand. As God continues to reveal actions that hinder or enhance divine presence, a series of acts that make the Israelites "clean" or "unclean" unfold. Leviticus 10:10–11 has already stated that priests were to "distinguish between the holy and the common, between the unclean and the clean" and to teach the people to do so as well. Since these four terms are the main emphases in Leviticus 11–27, it is important to understand what they mean.

Holiness means "set apart," "different," or "unique." God is holy in that He is different than humans in being, character, and actions. God cannot sin, but we can and do. Israel was holy in that they were set apart as uniquely called and privileged to serve the Lord. They were a kingdom of priests who shared God with the world (Exod. 19:5–6). Likewise, the church is holy to God and called to proclaim His excellence in all the earth (1 Pet. 2:9). Unholiness, on the other hand, amounted to any thought, motive, or deed that broke God's Word. Those who were unholy in this manner could not relate consistently to a holy God.

Clean and *unclean* are harder to define, since most current readers think of "sanitary" and "dirty" when they see these words. Such notions should be dismissed. A "clean" person was one ready for daily life and worship. An "unclean" person was not necessarily physically or morally

"Now therefore, if ye will obey my voice indeed, and keep my covenant, then ye shall be a peculiar treasure unto me above all people; for all the earth is mine: And ye shall be unto me a kingdom of priests, and an holy nation. These are the words which thou shalt speak unto the children of Israel" (Exod. 19:5–6, KJV).

"But ye are a chosen generation, a royal priesthood, an holy nation, a peculiar people; that ye should shew forth the praises of him who hath called you out of darkness into his marvellous light" (1 Pet. 2:9, KJV).

filthy. They were simply not cleared for traffic among other people. These laws only prohibited one's returning to normal life and worship when the person or the community could be harmed by doing so. An unclean person could usually become clean fairly quickly.

God required such careful living for several reasons. First, in the days before hospitals and medicines, quarantine was the best way to stop a disease from ravaging a community. Second, most of the laws helped to create a rested people who ate good diets. Third, these laws helped Israel to be different than their neighbors. Fourth, the laws helped develop a united community knit closely to their God. Doing the Lord's will made Israel a people committed to serving Him further.

UNCLEAN ANIMALS (LEV. 11)

Here the Lord separated animals which could be eaten (clean) from those that could not (unclean). The best-known example of an unclean animal is the pig (11:7), though camels (11:4), rabbits (11:6), and several sea creatures are mentioned as well (11:9–12). Various birds and insects are also declared unclean, as is the touching of dead bodies (11:13–43). Virtually all these animals and insects posed a health threat at that time. It is important to remember that Israel could have anything else! God gave them plenty to eat. They were sustained by a loving Lord.

God told the people to be holy and clean in these matters so that they might reflect His holiness (11:44). They were to be witnesses of and for God's purity. Only their relationship with the one living Lord made their holiness possible (11:45). As they did God's will they learned

Most, though not all, of the animals listed as "unclean" were scavengers at that time. Therefore, they carried impurities that could harm those who ate them. It is also possible that some of these animals were used in pagan worship rites. Eating them might have involved Israel in improper worship.

how to have an ever-closer relationship to their redeemer, the one who delivered them from slavery (11:45).

Of course, today's readers may wonder if we are supposed to keep these dietary laws today. The answer is no, for Christ declared all foods clean in Mark 7:19. Jesus did not set aside all Old Testament laws, but He did eliminate these. (More will be said on this subject in the section devoted to Leviticus 16.) Still, we can learn from this section, since God asks us to be set apart, holy, for His glory (see 1 Pet. 1:13–16). To nonbelievers, our commitment to Christ looks as odd as the dietary laws of Leviticus. Serving God according to His commands is the most logical thing to do, but the outside world rarely thinks so.

UNCLEANNESS DUE TO CHILDBIRTH (LEV. 12)

Readers often miss the point of this passage for three reasons. First, they think the Old Testament teaches that childbirth is dirty (12:1–3). Second, they conclude that this text considers giving birth to a girl dirtier than having a boy (12:4–5). Third, they get the impression that Moses considered childbirth a sin, for a sacrifice is commanded (12:6–8). It is true that the text tells women to stay home after having a boy, to stay home twice as long after delivering a girl, and to give a burnt offering when they return to society. The reasons just listed, however, are invalid.

All we need do to know that the Lord does not consider sexuality dirty or unacceptable is to read the Song of Solomon! God commands appropriate use of sexuality, but He does not consider it a necessary evil.

To begin with, the command to stay home amounted to a six-week pregnancy leave for the mother of a boy. This time of being unclean allowed her to recover and bond with her child without having to carry out other duties that took her into the community. Mothers having girls were given twice as long—probably because girl babies are quite often smaller than boys. Few societies have ever given women a twelve-week maternity leave! Some mothers may want to return to Moses' Law! The sacrifice made atonement for sins committed while on leave from society. It also marked the child's entrance into the community. God's Law called for special treatment for mothers, an entitlement women in most other ancient societies did not enjoy.

Perhaps because the King James Version translates "skin disease" as "leprosy," some readers think a specific malady is meant here. Various forms of leprosy may have existed in the ancient world, but a wider range of infections is intended here.

UNCLEANNESS DUE TO SKIN DISEASE (LEV. 13)

Leviticus 11–12 has already highlighted the protective nature of the cleanness laws. Both individuals and the whole community were secured through these standards. This principle also undergirds Leviticus 13, where infectious skin diseases and mildew are addressed.

Priests were charged with the responsibility of determining if a person had an infectious skin disease. Because an infected person had to be isolated (13:4) or even placed outside the community (13:45–46), priests were very careful in their diagnosis of such maladies. They were to conduct different investigations and treatments, depending on where the disease surfaced on the body (13:1–37). Hopefully, the problem was temporary, or nothing at all (13:16–17, 23, 28, 37–41). Only as a last resort were Israelites forced to live apart from others (13:45–46).

Similarly, clothing and leather materials damaged by mildew were checked (13:47–50), washed (13:54), and then reexamined (13:55–56). Only clothing that could not be salvaged had to be destroyed (13:57–58). Nearly identical laws for houses with spreading mildew appear in 14:33–57.

Though not all experts agree, these laws were intended to protect the community from outbreaks of fast-spreading infectious diseases. They were not given to pick on people with physical flaws. Whole communities could be wiped out by single epidemics in ancient times. Thus, these commands are as practical as those in Leviticus 12. God protected the whole nation by defining health risks and explaining how to deal with them.

BECOMING CLEAN AGAIN (LEV. 14)

This chapter proves that the purpose of chapter 13 is not to harass physically damaged persons. Here great pains are taken to explain how a previously unclean person could reenter community life. Restoration, not exile, was the goal at all times.

Two rituals marked the healed person's return to society. The first ceremony occurred outside the camp when it appeared that the person had recovered (14:1–7). Once pronounced clean, the individual could rejoin the community (14:8–9). The second ceremony took place at the sanctuary. It included the offering of sacrifices by the cleansed as well as an anointing of the healed by the priest (14:10–32). Both ceremonies were intended to bring the person back into full membership in the community. Healed persons were not to be treated with contempt, suspicion, or pity. They were to be treated as they had been before contracting the disease.

It is important to note that the text does not say that afflicted persons had done anything wrong. Their illness and time outside the community was not a result of sinful behavior.

"And there came a leper to him, beseeching him, and kneeling down to him, and saying unto him, If thou wilt, thou canst make me clean. And Jesus, moved with compassion, put forth his hand, and touched him, and saith unto him, I will; be thou clean. And as soon as he had spoken, immediately the leprosy departed from him, and he was cleansed. And he straitly charged him, and forthwith sent him away; And saith unto him, See thou say nothing to any man: but go thy way, show thyself to the priest, and offer for thy cleansing those things which Moses commanded, for a testimony unto them. But he went out, and began to publish it much, and to blaze abroad the matter, insomuch that Jesus could no more openly enter into the city, but was without in desert places: and they came to him from every quarter" (Mark 1:40–45, KJV).

Suffering often occurs even in the lives of faithful people. Such suffering may be like Christ's in that it can be on behalf of someone else. This redemptive suffering is not meaningless, for it offers a testimony that God is always worth serving, it keeps others from bearing that pain, and it builds character as we trust in the Lord, not ourselves (see 2 Cor. 12:1–10).

Serving God is not a magic charm against personal harm. Hard things happen to faithful people, as Moses, Jeremiah, Job, Jesus, Paul, and John could attest.

BODILY DISCHARGES THAT CAUSE UNCLEANNESS (LEV. 15)

Taken in context, it is likely that this chapter also isolates situations that can be dangerous to an individual or to the community. In fact, modern medicine agrees with this chapter's notion that diseases can be spread through body fluids. Therefore, we might not think it strange that this chapter mentions five instances that can make a person and those in close personal contact with that person clean or unclean.

First, 15:1–15 deals with unusual discharges from a man's sexual organ. Many experts think these verses refer to gonorrhea. If they are correct, then it is understandable for the text to warn against any contact with the discharge (15:4–12). Once healed of the disease, the man could bring a sin offering, be forgiven, and rejoin the community.

Second, 15:16–18 states that normal sexual activity resulting in a discharge of semen made both the man and woman unclean. They had to bathe and remain out of society until evening. This cleansing process allowed the couple time alone together and helped them avoid simple rashes and infections that could arise from normal sexual activity.

Third, 15:19–24 explains that a woman was to be considered unclean during her menstrual cycle. It also declares any man who had sex with the woman during this time unclean for seven days. As in the earlier passages, this command sought to limit transmitted diseases or infections. It also emphasized self-control by men.

Fourth, 15:25–30 discusses other discharges of blood in women. These instances were treated like the male discharges in 15:1–12, so it is likely the passage refers to serious infectious diseases. Women afflicted in this manner could receive forgiveness through giving a sin offering after their healing.

These commands were for Israel's own good (15:31–32). Each one protected the people from activities that may have proved harmful. Moses did not hate sexual expressions of love or women in general. Rather, he cautioned the people against the spread of disease. In the case of uncleanness after lovemaking, he may also have counseled nonsexual intimacy.

THE GOD WHO FORGIVES ALL SIN (LEV. 16)

This passage presents the heart of Leviticus' theology. Here we see God's holiness and mercy, Israel's need for forgiveness, and the book's emphasis on purity merge. These emphases come together in an annual observance called "the day of atonement." This holy day is known as Yom Kippur today. Any and all sins could be forgiven on that one special day. No clearer picture of God's grace and human faith in that grace appears in the Old Testament. Only the Cross surpasses it in the Bible.

The word *grace* means that through Christ we are given unmerited favor. That is, we are forgiven even though we do not deserve pardon. God's grace is as thorough as His holiness. Once given, it is never revoked (see 1 Pet. 1:3–9).

The Day of Atonement had to affect the priests before it could benefit the people. Leviticus 16:1–2 reminds readers of 10:1–3, for it warns against taking this ceremony lightly. It also sets forth the ritual's first point: the holiest room of the sanctuary could only be entered on this day, and only then by the high priest. Second, the high priest had to wear clothes different than his normal garments (16:3–5). He had to identify with the people. Third, the priest offered sacrifices for himself and his household (16:6). Fourth, he was to choose two goats for the main sacrifice. One was for the people's sins, and one was to be sent into the desert (16:7–10). Fifth, the priest had to kill a bull for his sins, then sprinkle some of its blood on the cover of the ark of the covenant (16:11–14). Thus, the priest's sins were forgiven.

Now the priest was ready to act on the people's behalf. First, he slaughtered one goat for the community's sins, then sprinkled its blood on the ark's cover (16:15). This act cleansed the Holy Place and Most Holy Place of Israel's sins. Second, the priest atoned for the altar by sprinkling blood upon it (16:18–19). Any insincerity in worship was thereby cleansed.

The Day of Atonement differed from the other offerings in that it covered every type of sin. It also covered all sins committed during a year. Thus, it was the most comprehensive of the sacrifices.

Third, and most importantly, the priest placed his hands on the live goat's head, transferred the people's sins to the head of the animal, and sent the goat to the desert (16:20–22). *All* the people's sins were on the goat. No condemnation or guilt remained. God's grace and mercy overcame sin and guilt and shame. Joy, reconciliation, and fellowship with God resulted. This substitutionary sacrifice was accepted by God in place of Israel's sins. Only by faith could the nation believe this was true, for it seemed too good to be true.

Israel was supposed to prepare carefully for this day. It was a Sabbath set apart for special observance (16:29–34). The people were to take the day seriously and by faith receive God's pardon. Otherwise they cut themselves off from God's chosen means for their forgiveness.

Of course, Christians do not offer sacrifices now. The reason is not that the Old Testament sacrifices were useless, the mere results of misguided legalism. After all, God commanded these sacrifices, and God promised pardon through them. Rather, the reason is that they were sequential, not permanent, and were preparatory for a conclusive, greater sacrifice. That greater sacrifice w 's Jesus' death on the cross.

Hebrews 9:7–12 states th... .. problem with the Day of Atonement w.as hat it had to occur every year. Worshipers' conscic... .s could not be cleared permanently. Therefore, the sacrifices of Leviticus applied until Christ made a once-for-all atonement for sins. In this way Leviticus 16 prepared people of the first century to believe in Jesus. It also helped amaze them at God's grace. The fact that Jesus' death was all the burnt offerings, guilt, sin, and Day of Atonement sacrifices rolled into one must have staggered early Christians' imaginations. It may also have caused them to bow in awe and wonder, a posture we would do well to emulate.

"Neither by the blood of goats and calves, but by his own blood he entered in once into the holy place, having obtained eternal redemption for us. For if the blood of bulls and of goats, and the ashes of an heifer sprinkling the unclear sanctifieth to the purifyin of the flesh: How...uch more shall the blood of Christ, who through the eternal Spirit offered himself without spot to God, purge your conscience from dead works to serve the living God" (Heb. 9:12–14, KJV).

God gave rules and guidelines that would keep His people healthy and convey to them the fact that they were to separate themselves from those things that made them unclean. Moreover, when they became defiled, God provided a way for them to come to Him for cleansing. The Day of Atonement was given as an occasion on which the high priest offered sacrifices to cleanse the priests, the tabernacle, and the people. Sins committed the previous year were forgiven.

QUESTIONS TO GUIDE YOUR STUDY

1. In Israel, what was the importance of distinguishing between "clean" and "unclean"?
2. What was the practical import of the law regarding uncleanness due to childbirth?
3. What were the laws regarding skin diseases and mildew given to guard against?
4. Describe the Day of Atonement and its significance.

Part Four
The God Who Requires
Holiness: Leviticus 17–27

Leviticus 17–27 emphasizes that holy living was Israel's proper response to God's loving holiness. Israel was to be different than the Canaanite peoples (18:1–5). They were to be holy because their God is holy (19:2; 20:7, 26), and had set them apart as a holy nation (20:26). Here God makes holy rules based on His personal holiness (21:23), makes the rules holy (22:16), makes the people holy (22:31–33), and makes certain festivals holy (23:1–25:54). Clearly, holiness saturates these texts, and just as clearly Israel can only achieve holiness by believing in God and obeying God's Word.

THE HOLY PLACE AND BLOOD (LEV. 17)

This chapter reinforces the tabernacle as the place God has chosen for proper sacrifices. It also discusses how to guard against practices that might undermine the offering of correct sacrifices and a commitment to the sanctuary's importance. To do so it addresses both worship and "typical life" in a way that helps readers know that the two cannot be separated.

Leviticus 17:1–9 reminded Israel that the central sanctuary is *the only place* where sacrifices were to be brought. Those who sacrificed elsewhere were to be cut off from the people (17:3–4). Israel had been sacrificing in open fields (17:5). Some of the people had been bringing offerings to idols (17:7). Such actions had to stop (17:8–9). Bringing their offerings to one place, then, was designed to eliminate the

"But you are to seek the place the LORD your God will choose from among all your tribes to put his Name there for his dwelling. To that place you must go; there bring your burnt offerings and sacrifices, your tithes and special gifts, what you have vowed to give and your freewill offerings, and the firstborn of your herds and flocks" (Deut. 12:5–6).

"And almost all things are by the law purged with blood; and without shedding of blood is no remission" (Heb. 9:22, KJV).

temptation to worship in ways that could lead to outright paganism.

Leviticus 17:10–12 insists that Israel not eat blood. This command guarded the sanctity of worship as well, since it set apart animal blood for use in sacrifices alone. Blood made atonement, so it was not to be treated as a common product.

Leviticus 17:13–16 regulated hunting procedures in keeping with 17:1–12. Israelites could kill animals as needed but they could never drink the blood, nor could they use the animal as a sacrifice. Even their daily activities were governed by spiritual principles. Every detail of their lives was to be integrated with their faith. Their existence was supposed to be a unified whole, not a series of segmented parts.

HOLINESS AND SEXUAL RELATIONS (LEV. 18)

Leviticus 18 moves even deeper into the Israelites' personal lives. Living as God's holy people included avoiding sexual practices done in worship and in daily life by the Egyptians and Canaanites (18:1–3). Israel had to obey God's standards, not those of the people around them (18:3–4). The people stood between the worldview they left behind in Egypt and the one they would discover when they got to Canaan. If they wanted to live a long time in the Promised Land (18:5), then they had to live differently from those people who worshiped idols. They could not serve lust and God at the same time. Therefore, the chapter addresses five matters related to sexuality, ethics, and worship.

Experts claim that as many as one-third of all girls and one-fourth of all boys in America are victims of sexual abuse during their adolescence. This plague leads to physical pain, difficulty in marriage, and the loss of trust, among other horrible results. Christians must support the elimination of this evil through appropriate means.

First, Leviticus 18:6 states that Israelites could not have sexual relations with "close relatives," a term 18:7–19 then defines. These prohibitions against incest demonstrate God's opposition to sexual abuse. Indeed, these verses are virtually the sole place where this horrible crime is discussed in the Bible, so they are vital for protecting victims today. These laws also state God's opposition to the misuse of authority for sexual "gain," the wrecking of relational trust in families, and the use of any person, male or female, as an object of satisfying wicked desires. There was no place for such detestable acts then, nor is there any place for them in decent society now.

Second, God reminded the people that adultery was forbidden (18:20). Adultery defiles its participants, blurs family lines, severely damages or even destroys spousal trust, and betrays a person's relationship with God. Adultery is the one possible (not obligatory) reason for divorce that Jesus explicitly mentioned (see Matt. 5:31–32; 19:1–12). Clearly, marital fidelity is a serious matter.

This text denounces child sacrifice, as does Genesis 22:1–19. Thus, any child sacrifice was wrong in Israel, so Jephthah's sacrifice of his daughter consisted of a rash vow followed by murder (see Judg. 11:1–40).

Third, Israel's children could not be offered to Molech, an ancient god to whom children were sacrificed by fire (18:21). Israel's children were not fodder for nondeities. Neither were they to be disposed of when they were inconvenient to raise. Personal holiness includes parental responsibility.

Fourth, homosexuality was prohibited (18:22). Some religions used homosexual prostitutes as part of their worship, so this law opposed such practices. It also covered homosexuality outside of religious settings. Homosexuality, like the sins already mentioned in this chapter, destroys the family unit God instituted and promised to bless in the Promised Land. Romans 1:18–32 lists homosexual behavior as an improper

The Bible clearly teaches that sex is a heterosexual activity that is appropriate only for adult men and women married to one another. All other expressions violate God's standards.

"And Jesus answered him, The first of all the commandments is, Hear, O Israel; The Lord our God is one Lord: And thou shalt love the Lord thy God with all thy heart, and with all thy soul, and with all thy mind, and with all thy strength: this is the first commandment. And the second is like, namely this, Thou shalt love thy neighbour as thyself. There is none other commandment greater than these" (Mark 12:29–31, KJV).

activity in a fallen, corrupt world. Homosexual acts are sins that can be cleansed, but they are still sins.

Fifth, God denounces bestiality (18:23). Again, there were ancient religions that incorporated such practices. Egypt was a noticeable case in point. Bestiality in any culture is a sign that sexuality has gone terribly wrong. At the very least it breaks the family bonds forged when God determined that Eve, not some animal, completed Adam (see Gen. 2:18–25).

Participating in these forbidden sexual practices would jeopardize Israel's future in the Promised Land. Indeed, God decided to displace the Canaanites because of their corrupt theology and ethics (18:24–28). Israelites who disagreed with these principles were to be "cut off" from the community, lest sin spread (18:29–30). Vigilance was needed for Israel to obey God's commands when faced with competing worldviews. Only commitment to God's revealed Word would help them withstand the temptation to live like the countries near them.

HOLINESS IN EVERY AREA OF LIFE (LEV. 19)

God's commands continue to expand, gradually addressing more life situations. So far the nation has been told how to behave at the sanctuary and in their homes. Now they are instructed in how to act in a variety of other situations. As in the Ten Commandments (see Exod. 20:1–17), respect for God and neighbor frame these laws (19:2, 18), as does God's past relationship with Israel (19:3, 4, 10, 12, etc.). God's holiness is the basis for these laws (19:2), and it is the only reason Israel has the privilege of being a holy people (19:37).

Between the basis (19:2) and expectation of holiness (19:2, 37), virtually every one of the Ten Commandments are repeated and/or explained. As usual, idolatry is prohibited and quality worship of God ordered (19:4–8, 30). Commands to shun divination, sorcery, mediums, and spiritists also appear (19:26, 31). Occult activities amount to serving false gods. Consulting psychics and mediums is the same as seeking advice from a false prophet. Israel had to trust in God and God's Word—and nothing else—for their daily living.

Other laws here deal with how to treat others. Chief among these is 19:18: "Do not seek revenge or bear a grudge against one of your people, but love your neighbor as yourself. I am the LORD." Israel's "neighbors" included people of foreign descent, not just their ethnic kin (19:33–34). Jesus told the people of His day that a Samaritan was a Jewish person's neighbor (see Luke 10:25–37). He summarized the law by citing this passage and Deuteronomy 6:4–9 (see Mark 12:28–34). Israel was to demonstrate their love for God in part by showing love to one another and to strangers. Love is the heart of the law.

Loving one another allowed the people to avoid stealing, bearing false witness, oppressing the poor, or perverting justice (19:9–16). It combated sins that begin in the heart, where unholy attitudes and actions originate (19:17). It eliminated sins against foreigners, family, and business associates (19:20–36). Clearly, no person stood outside the definition of "neighbor." All persons deserve our respect, love, and just treatment.

HOLINESS AND PUNISHMENTS FOR SIN (LEV. 20)

God's holiness included more than loving and instructing Israel. It also entailed setting punishment for those who rebelled against the divinely revealed principles already elaborated. Without consequences for sin, God's imperatives would have become God's preferences. This does not mean God had changed. The same God who delivered Israel in Exodus 1–15 judged Israel for making a golden idol in Exodus 32–34. God's character remained intact: a perfect blend of love, holiness, justice, and mercy.

The seriousness of the sins described in chapters 18–19 becomes plain here. Anyone who gave a child to Molech (18:21) deserved death (20:1–5). Child sacrifice was murder. Persons who were or turned to mediums were to be sentenced to death (20:6; 20:27). The same was true of adulterers (18:20; 20:10), sexual abusers (18:6–19; 20:11–12), sexually active homosexuals (18:22; 20:13), or participants in bestiality (18:23; 20:15–16). Other sins were punished by the perpetrators being cut off from the community. These transgressions included sexual acts of various sorts (20:17–21). Again, part of God's intent for these commands was to help Israel avoid gross sins done by the Canaanites (20:22–24). Israel could not be like those who did not serve God and manage to be a holy nation.

People often wonder if the punishments listed here are too severe. They typically state that the New Testament shows more grace than Leviticus, then forget these laws. Or, they try to retain the laws somehow, but are not sure on what grounds. This subject is important for those who think the whole Bible is God's Word. It is also vital because many of the subjects covered here are seldom discussed elsewhere in the Scriptures.

Christians today have no right to impose death for the sins mentioned here. No nation operates under biblical law now. Still, believers must note that such actions are wrong and are therefore detrimental to any community and any person. These sins can be forgiven as a person repents. But Paul warns in 1 Corinthians 6:9–11 that persons who rebelliously practice these things will suffer spiritual death. They will not inherit the kingdom of God. The church cannot put persons to death, but it can and should warn of spiritual death and proclaim the good news of cleansing from sin and eternal life through Jesus Christ.

"But I will forewarn you whom ye shall fear: Fear him, which after he hath killed hath power to cast into hell; yea, I say unto you, Fear him" (Luke 12:5, KJV).

HOLINESS AND THE PRIESTS' WORK (LEV. 21–22)

More than anyone else, the priests were to be concerned with God's holiness in the community. As leaders, they had to be even more careful about and knowledgeable of God's ways. Therefore, these chapters set forth rules for priests that complement those commands already found in Leviticus 1–10. Six areas are covered here, each one making certain that the priests live by high standards.

First, Leviticus 21:1–9 discusses standards for mourning and marriage. Priests were not to touch dead bodies, except in the case of their father, mother, or unmarried sister (21:1–4). Nor were they to cut their hair or beard, which was probably part of the mourning practices of the surrounding nations (21:5–6). Priests were to marry only virgins. Unlike the rest of the populace, they were forbidden to wed even a widow

(21:7; see 21:13–15). This law underscored the strenuous nature of the priests' calling. It set them apart from the people.

Second, Leviticus 21:10–15 explains standards for the high priest. He had to keep his special garments (see Exod. 28) clean and intact (21:10). He could not touch even the dead bodies of his parents (21:11–12), and he had to marry a virgin (21:13–15). As the chief priest he had to adhere to requirements higher than those of regular priests. Corruption was to be avoided, for it would be a spiritual plague on the nation.

Third, Leviticus 21:16–24 states what physical handicaps were unsuitable for a practicing priest. Virtually every one of the problems mentioned here would render the individual incapable of carrying out a priest's assigned task. A priest's job was physically hard, for it required a good bit of cutting, carrying, and lifting. Handicapped persons were allowed to eat of the holy food, so they were not expelled from the priestly tribe. It is just that they could not accomplish the necessary tasks for helping the people.

Fourth, Leviticus 22:1–9 describes the circumstances under which priests could not eat the holy food, or offerings. The main reason for such exclusion was uncleanness of the type mentioned in Leviticus 11–15. Any priest made temporarily or permanently unclean was excluded, and anyone who broke this law was to be executed (22:9). God's means for securing forgiveness could not be treated as if it were merely a priest's meal ticket.

Fifth, Leviticus 22:10–16 identifies who could share the priests' portion of the holy food. Only close family members had this privilege. Anyone eating sacred food by accident could be forgiven, but even an inadvertent offense was to be treated as serious. Of course, this law says nothing against sharing food with the needy. David received some sacred bread when under duress (see 1 Sam. 21:1–6), which Jesus approved in Luke 6:1–5. No doubt Leviticus deals with normal, not extreme, situations.

Sixth, Leviticus 22:17–33 defines acceptable and unacceptable sacrifices. As Leviticus 1–7 has already stated, only choice animals were to be brought to the altar. Sin was costly. It was not to be treated lightly, nor was forgiveness to be considered as cheaply purchased. The priests had to make certain that Israel understood what was at stake at the altar. Just as God's priests had to be serious about their calling, qualifications, and tasks, so the people were supposed to take their personal confession and sacrificing seriously. Anything less dishonored God and placed souls in jeopardy. Anything less also placed the priests in a weakened financial position.

One might consider these laws harsh, or confining. One must remember, however, that the God who loved Israel devotedly made these rules (22:31–33). God's love led to Israel's holiness as much as it led to their very existence. Love defined boundaries and consequences here just as surely as it produced freedom in Exodus.

THE SABBATH AND HOLY DAYS (LEV. 23)

God rules history in power, mercy, majesty, and holiness. This principle has been evident in Scripture since Genesis 1–3. Though self-existent before days and seasons begin to mark time, God creates and guides events that unfold

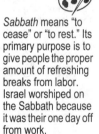

Sabbath means "to cease" or "to rest." Its primary purpose is to give people the proper amount of refreshing breaks from labor. Israel worshiped on the Sabbath because it was their one day off from work.

in human history. In this way God makes sure that time and events are meaningful. Nowhere in the Bible is God's concern to make occasions momentous more striking than in Leviticus 23–25. Here the Lord sets aside holy days and feasts that mark ancient and contemporary history as more than the mere passing of hours. The Sabbath introduced this idea as early as Genesis 2:2–3. The institution of festivals in Exodus 12:1–28, 23:14–17, and 34:18–25 furthered the concept. Now Moses formalizes the notion still further.

Sabbath observance was the foundation for all other special times. Part of the very fabric of creation (Gen. 2:2–3) and part of the Ten Commandments (Exod. 20:1–17), the Sabbath was a weekly reminder that the holy people served a holy God (23:3). The word *Sabbath* means "to cease." Stopping labor one day a week showed that the Israelites were no more slaves to their own ambitions than they were to the Egyptians. Resting also gave them the time to draw nearer to the Lord.

Many oral traditions were added to the Sabbath laws. People were told how many steps they could walk on the Sabbath, even whether or not one could carry false teeth on the Sabbath. These traditions are not part of Scripture, and should not be cited as evidence that Sabbath keeping is sheer legalism.

There has been a great deal of misunderstanding about the Sabbath. People today often hear of rules and regulations added to the Scriptures' teaching about this day of rest. Jesus said that the Sabbath was made for people, not people for the Sabbath (Mark 2:27). By this He meant that the day of rest was God's gift for weary people. It was a time of restoration for body and soul. Thus, He freely healed and met personal needs on the Sabbath (Mark 2:23–3:6). At the same time, these incidents prove that Jesus changed His normal pattern of rest to engage in these activities. Jesus defined rest; He did not do away with it.

Today many Christians either act as if Jesus did away with rest, as if the Pharisees were right about it, or that the word *Sabbath* means "to worship." Those who take the latter attitude seem to think they have kept the Sabbath if they have been to church. The rest of the time they can work or recreate as long and hard as they wish. In this way they really act like those who believe the Sabbath has been repealed.

How may one keep the Sabbath today? First, it must be remembered that the Sabbath concept is one day of rest in seven. For many this day could be Sunday, but for ministers and persons on alternative work schedules this is not feasible. Such persons should rest another day. Second, all activities that drain a person should be avoided. Alternatively, those deeds that heal and restore should be encouraged. Third, time with the Lord and family ought to characterize the Sabbath as well. If Sundays allow for these blessings, then all is fine and good. If not, then church attendance should not be forsaken, but another day of rest should be chosen. Surely our weary, stressed-filled world could use this gift of God.

The first Passover occurred the night God killed Egypt's firstborn, which was the event that caused Pharaoh to release Israel. It was reenacted each year, with a large emphasis on teaching children the history of God's work on Israel's behalf.

Passover was as connected to the Exodus as the Sabbath to creation. The first of the spring festivals, this observance marked the start of Israel's year (23:4), just as the Exodus marked the beginning of Israel's nationhood (see Exod. 12:1–28). Passover reminded Israel that God delivered them to be a holy people. The Feast of Unleavened Bread occurred at the same time as Passover, and commemorated God's sparing of Israel from slavery. During this week-long event the people were to rest, offer sacrifices, and rejoice at their deliverance (23:6–8). Like the other festivals, Passover was an important time for families to instruct one another in their faith (see Exod. 12:24–28).

Jesus chose the Passover to institute the Lord's Supper (see Luke 22:7–23). He used the unleavened bread to symbolize His body, and the fruit of the vine to symbolize His blood. In this way He linked the Lord's saving work in the Old and New Testaments. He also portrayed His death as the final saving act of the Scriptures. No greater sacrifice is needed or possible.

The Feast of Weeks (23:15–22) was observed seven weeks after the firstfruits of harvest were gathered (23:9–14). Israel was to give God credit for the crops that grew in the Promised Land. The Feast of Weeks itself was a time of rest, sacrifice, and taking care of the poor (23:22). It reminded the people of God's goodness and prodded them toward gratitude, generosity, and openness of heart.

The Feast of Trumpets and Day of Atonement began the fall festivals (23:23–32). The former event was a time of rest and alerted the nation that the great once-a-year offering for sin was about to be made (23:23–25). Nine days after the Feast of Trumpets (23:26), the Day of Atonement occurred. It, too, was a time of rest and reflection. As was discussed in the comments on Leviticus 16, this day was the one on which all Israel's sins for the past year were pardoned. Prior to Christ's death on the cross, no day was more important for the securing of God's forgiveness.

Having received pardon for their sins, five days later the people reenacted the Exodus and celebrated their role as God's people by observing the Feast of Tabernacles (23:33–44). This festival required the people to stay in makeshift, lean-to sorts of dwellings while the feast lasted (23:42–43). In this way they recalled how their ancestors lived in the days after leaving Egypt.

Each of these special times connected Israel's past and present. The people were to live as if the same God who saved and sustained them in the past would do so in the present. Today God's people can do the same by marking these events, as well as by paying attention to and celebrating Christmas, Easter, Pentecost, and other special days. Staying linked to the past will give assurance, peace, confidence, and hope in the present.

THE HOLINESS OF GOD'S PRESENCE AND GOD'S NAME (LEV. 24)

Everything about the tabernacle was intended to remind Israel of God's presence. The altar and ark of the covenant proved that God was present to forgive. The tabernacle itself showed that the holy God dwelled among the holy people. God's presence alone ensured that Israel could survive.

Leviticus 24:1–9 illustrates this concept as well. Israel was to provide oil for constantly burning lamps and bread to be placed before the Lord always. The oil lamps possibly represented both God's presence and the ceaseless prayers of the people to their living Lord. Perhaps the bread demonstrated God's sustenance on the one hand and the people's commitment to their priests on the other. The priests were allowed to eat this bread (24:9)

Leviticus 24:10–23 emphasizes the importance of honoring the holiness of God's name. Of course, the third commandment (Exod. 20:7) warns that God will punish those who take His name lightly ("in vain" KJV). God's name could

Many persons think that avoiding certain kinds of cursing keeps one from taking God's name in vain. While cursing should be avoided, it is also necessary to not take any part of God's character lightly or to speak in God's name when God has not told you to speak.

not be abused in anyway, for in the Old Testament a person's "name" was the same thing as his or her "person" or "character." Thus, anyone abusing God's name was also abusing God and His reputation.

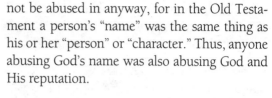

Israel's laws were to protect every level of society. It was blind to class, race, or status. Not even kings were above the Law (see Deut. 17:14–20).

Therefore, a person who spoke against God was put to death (24:10–16, 23). This offense was considered as detrimental to the community as taking life (24:17). When serious crimes were committed the punishment was to fit the crime, which is what the phrase "eye for eye, tooth for tooth" (24:18–20) means. The notion is not revenge, but fairness for all people, regardless of their parentage (24:22). Where God's presence is appreciated, justice will prevail. Where God's name is taken in vain, one can expect injustice born out of a lack of respect for the highest authority.

A HOLY GOD AND HOLY YEARS (LEV. 25)

Two final sacred times constitute God's most radical commands of rest, renewal, and forgiveness. First, every seventh year the land was to rest. It was to lie fallow (25:1–6). Whatever grew by itself could be consumed (25:6). Israel was to trust that God would bless them sufficiently in the years leading up to the Sabbath year so that they could survive for this one special year (25:18–22). The blessings they had received proved that their God, the Creator, could sustain them. This Sabbath year restored the land, of course, as anyone familiar with crop rotation will attest. Perhaps more importantly, it taught Israel that life does not consist simply of work, making money, power, success, and appetite. Rather, individual and national fulfillment consisted in being God's holy people.

Debt can be a crushing load to individuals, families, and churches. It should only be undertaken under the most necessary of circumstances (see Rom. 13:8), and it should not be used to keep anyone in poverty.

Second, every fiftieth year was to be a Jubilee year. At that time debts were to be forgiven, indentured servants released, and ancestral lands returned to their original owners (25:8–18). In other words, the economy was given rest. This observance rested on four convictions:

1. Israel must fear God and refuse to take advantage of one another (25:17).
2. Israel must have faith that God will provide (25:18–22).
3. Israel must realize that the Promised Land belongs to the Creator, who divides it by grace, not by merit or social standing (25:23–24).
4. Israel must understand that they belong to God. Therefore, human beings are not property in any full or permanent sense (25:35–55).

These standards indicate that the poor and helpless were to be helped in a holy nation (25:35–38; see 23:22). Other countries had release laws during this era, so surely the holy nation should as well. The poor were not to be kept down. To move up, they needed land, financial solvency, freedom (25:39–55), and opportunity. The poor were not to take advantage of the situation, but neither were the rich. Israel was supposed to be a community of caring, responsible persons, not a collection of greedy, profit-driven, oppressive individuals. God redeemed them for higher things, even as He promised to meet their needs.

BLESSINGS, CONSEQUENCES, AND THE HOLY PEOPLE (LEV. 26)

Leviticus 26 calls Israel to action. It sets forth potential blessings and consequences based on their faithfulness to the covenant God has

"Moses and the elders of Israel commanded the people: 'Keep all these commands that I give you today. When you have crossed the Jordan into the land the LORD your God is giving you, set up some large stones and coat them with plaster'" (Deut. 27:1–2).

"However, if you do not obey the LORD your God and do not carefully follow all his commands and decrees I am giving you today, all these curses will come upon you and overtake you" (Deut. 28:15).

offered them. Either Israel must accept God's gracious standards or lose the opportunity to do so. Thus, the chapter unfolds in two specific parts: the offering of blessing, and the threat of punishment.

Leviticus 26:1–13 promises Israel total success in the Promised Land if they obey God's Word (see 26:3). The same kind, saving God who gave them dignity (26:13) will establish them in the land. What must they do? By now the answer is clear. They must believe in one God (26:1) and worship Him as they have been commanded (26:2). What will be the results? They will enjoy a fruitful land (26:3–5), peace (26:6–8), and, most importantly, a genuine and transforming relationship with the Lord (26:9–13). God's past acts on their behalf should reassure them of His future kind intentions (26:13).

On the other hand, Leviticus 26:14–46 describes the consequences of spiritual infidelity. If Israel is disobedient, then the Lord will withhold the land's blessing (26:14–16), defeat them in war (26:17), make the land hostile (26:21–22), and send plagues upon them (26:23–26). Why? To chasten their pride (26:19) and help them listen to the Lord again (26:14, 18, 21, 23, 27). If these disciplinary punishments fail to make Israel come to their senses, then God will drive them from the Promised Land (26:27–35). Only a frightened remnant will remain (26:36–39).

Even this last terrible punishment will be for the purpose of bringing Israel to repentance. When out of the land, in need, and desperate if the people pray to the Lord, He will hear them, forgive them, and restore them (26:40–45). God's discipline always occurs to amend behavior, for

God's desire is to bless, not punish. If this were not so, the covenant would never have been offered in the first place. God is holy *and* gracious at the same time.

Israel's history can be examined fruitfully against the background of this chapter and its companion text, Deuteronomy 27–28. Both the Old Testament historical books and the prophetic books follow the views of Leviticus 26. When Israel obeyed God, they enjoyed God's presence and God's blessings. When they did not do so, the Lord disciplined and warned them. Eventually God drove them from the land because of their stubborn rebellion against the one who loved them most (see 2 Kings 17; Jer. 52). Passages such as Joshua 24, Judges 2, Nehemiah 9, and Psalms 105–106 reflect the view of history found in Leviticus 26. Thus, keen Bible students should look for these developments when reading the rest of the Old Testament.

THE HOLY PEOPLE KEEP THEIR WORD (LEV. 27)

Leviticus closes with commands related to Israel's trustworthiness. God asks for a commitment in chapter 26, and chapter 27 addresses the truthfulness of their speech. Without dedication to promise keeping and truth telling, their pledges to do God's will must prove hollow. More specifically, this passage deals with promises to give income to the Lord's work.

Several ways to give extra money to the Lord appear here:

1. Persons may dedicate themselves (27:1–8).
2. Persons may dedicate an animal (27:9–13).

God is more impressed with the heart with which we give and the financial sacrifice we make than the exact amount we give. Jesus' observations about the widow who gave all she had prove this point (see Mark 12:41–44).

3. Persons may dedicate houses or land (27:14–25).

Nothing that was already required, such as the firstborn or the tithe, could be considered a special (dedicated) offering (27:26–33).

The Bible is not shy about asking for offerings. One of the more extended discussions of the subject is found in 2 Corinthians 8–9, where Paul urges the church to give generously for a good cause. Believers should see giving as a privilege. When they pledge to give, they ought to do as they promise.

CONCLUSION: LEVITICUS FOR TODAY

Today's church can learn much from this great book. First, we can marvel at what a wonderful place Israel would have been had these laws been followed. Fairness, forgiveness, safety, and hope would have filled the land. Injustice, abuse, rivalry, violence, and blasphemy would have been absent. We should either use these laws or work to enact statutes based upon them.

Second, we can gain a greater sense of Christ's death for us. His sacrifice on the cross amounted to all the burnt offerings, sin, guilt, fellowship, and Day of Atonement sacrifices that ever needed to be offered. He took our place and the place of every animal substitute ever needed. Forgiveness is now complete, not sequential. We can know that our pardon and cleansing is permanently complete.

Third, we can be a chastened people when we do not obey the Lord's Word. Revelation 2–3, Paul's epistles, and the General Epistles all testify to the fact that God disciplines individuals and churches. Only fidelity to the Lord and the fellowship with Him which it brings can truly make the church God's holy people. Only faithfulness born of God's power brings God's blessings. Only repentance from sin can bring us back from the spiritual deserts we create for ourselves.

Fourth, we can be a hopeful people. God desires to bless us, and He does so every day. God guides us in holy living. We can count on His help in this life, and we can expect an even brighter future in eternity. Leviticus teaches that great things lie in store for people who are holy as God is holy (Lev. 11:44).

■ *God was not content to allow Israel to simply*
■ *avoid sin. In these chapters, the people*
■ *learned how they could move toward moral*
■ *excellence. They were to demonstrate these*
■ *qualities by the ways they responded to God*
■ *and how they treated one another. The cove-*
■ *nant concluded with commands about what*
■ *belongs to God.*

QUESTIONS TO GUIDE YOUR STUDY

1. Why was it so important to allow sacrifices to be made in only one place?
2. Why did God institute the Sabbath?
3. What was the importance of holy years?
4. What benefits can contemporary Christians derive from the study and practice of the principles in Leviticus?

THE GOD WHO EXPECTS FAITHFULNESS: NUMBERS

Faith is the key to success in any new spiritual venture. Individuals, families, and churches alike need to trust God's Word and God's instructions if they want to honor the Lord. Indeed, only unbelief can stop those who are truly called by God to a specific task.

Numbers follows Leviticus chronologically. Israel had been at Mount Sinai for a year (see Num. 9:1–14), receiving God's gracious standards for their community. Now it was time for the people to march to Canaan and conquer the Promised Land. Israel had strong leadership. They had a divinely revealed code by which to live. God gave them a new sense of national identity and promised them a fine future. Israel knew God's character. They knew what pleased and displeased Him. Greatness was well within their grasp because of the grace of their great God.

Tragically, these hopeful possibilities were shattered through a lack of faith in God. In a crucial moment, the people failed to believe God and thus forfeited their opportunity to enter the Promised Land. They then added bitterness and divisiveness to their lack of faith. All this in spite of the fact that God not only expected faithfulness; He deserved it. God gave Israel the Promised Land in due time, yet only to the next generation—which trusted Him.

THE GOD WHO GUIDES AND INSPIRES: NUMBERS 1:1–10:10

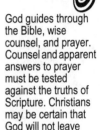

The same God who revealed the truths in Leviticus continued to communicate with Moses now (1:1). A year had passed since the Exodus (1:2); it was time to move forward. Thus, God gave marching orders in chapters 1–4, then stated how Israel could remain pure and holy and as they went forward in 5:1–10:10. Along the way, the Lord inspired Israel to keep the Passover (9:1–14) and begin the process of conquest (9:15–10:10).

God guides through the Bible, wise counsel, and prayer. Counsel and apparent answers to prayer must be tested against the truths of Scripture. Christians may be certain that God will not leave them without guidance.

THE HOLY PEOPLE READY TO MARCH (NUM. 1–4)

God gave Moses five specific tasks in Numbers 1–4. First, God ordered a census taken of all men twenty years old or more so that Israel's fighting force might be organized (1:1–46). This force represented Israel's status as an emerging nation. They were no longer slaves. It indicated that God would bless Israel as they worked at doing what the Lord commanded and empowered them to do.

Second, God instructed Moses to exclude the Levites from the census, for they cared for the tabernacle (1:47–50). The Levites guarded the nation's sense of God's holiness (1:51–53). Therefore, though they were not fighting, the Levites had a special role in protecting Israel.

Third, the Lord told Moses how to arrange the tribes when they camped and when they marched (2:1–34). What is striking about both situations is that the symbols of God's presence had the highest visibility. When Israel stopped, the sanctuary was to rest in the middle of the square encampment (2:2). When the people marched, persons carrying the ark were to lead three tribes, those bearing the tabernacle three tribes, and those conveying the tabernacle furnishings six tribes (2:17). God's presence could never be forgotten or taken for granted. God's presence meant He led both from a distance and close at hand.

Fourth, the Lord separated the tribe of Levi and assigned them specific tasks (3:1–51). Most important were Aaron and his sons, since they were to be "the anointed priests" (3:3; see Exod. 28–29). All the Levites were significant, though, for they were specifically chosen from among the Israelites to serve God. They belonged to the Lord (3:11–13, 45), so they were a separated group within the holy nation. They were not better than the rest of the people. But they were held to higher standards than the others (see Lev. 21–22).

Fifth, God chose from among the Levites specific clans to carry the ark, the tabernacle, and the tabernacle furnishings (4:1–33). With these instructions given, the Lord told Moses to count the Levites (4:34–39). Once again, God guided Israel to respect His holiness, which was their hope for success and glory (4:17–20). Israel could march in confidence, knowing that Moses had led them to obey the Lord (see 1:54; 2:34; 3:16, 51; 4:49). Indeed, obedience and instruction existed in equal measure at this point in time.

THE HOLY PEOPLE SPIRITUALLY PREPARED (NUM. 5:1–10:10)

With marching orders in place, God guided Israel's spiritual preparations in this section. To fulfill the commands set forth in Leviticus 11–25, the Lord told the people to move unclean persons outside the camp (5:1–4), to make restitution for wrongs done to God and others (5:5–10), and to expose adultery and false accusations of adultery (5:11–31). Each step reminded Israel of their calling as a holy people serving a holy God (see Exod. 19:5–6; Lev. 11:44–45). Each step demonstrated their commitment to being different than the people they were sent to displace (see Lev. 17–25).

Women were not always treated fairly in ancient cultures. God's law protected them from false accusations, unjust divorces, and financial destitution. Of course, Israel did not always obey these laws.

Though all the people were holy to the Lord, some Israelites were called to express their desire for personal and community holiness in public, formal ways. For instance, men or women could choose to become Nazirites. These persons abstained from fermented drinks, let their hair grow during their committed time, and avoided dead bodies while under their vow (6:1–8). Their commitment could last for either a short or long time (6:9–21). Samson is the Bible's best-known Nazirite (see Judg. 13–16). Readers of this text who are familiar with the Samson accounts can easily judge how carefully he did or did not adhere to Nazirite standards. The Nazirites' commitments demonstrated the high value these persons placed on serving their God.

Israel's leaders were called upon to show their special devotion to God by bringing offerings (7:1–89). These gifts were to be used in the work of the tabernacle (7:4). Elders from every tribe but Levi, which was set apart for special service, brought generous gifts. This giving spirit approximated that of Exodus 35:1–36:7, when the people gave so much they had to be restrained from bringing more. How many congregations today have *that* problem? These persons saw giving as a privilege, and they gave with all their heart.

The Levites testified to God's worthiness by giving their lives to Him (8:1–26). This commitment was not specifically greater than that of the leaders in chapter 7, since it was required of them by the Lord. Nonetheless, their obedience meant that they had to depend on Israel to bring proper sacrifices for their families to be fed. They had to adhere to a higher standard of conduct than the typical Israelite, and they had to teach and admonish the very people upon whom they depended for their livelihood. All of this meant that they had to trust the Lord in every detail of their lives. In other words, ministers' lives have not changed much over the past three thousand years!

Israel's setting apart of the Levites required ritual washing (8:5–7), offering sacrifices (8:8–14), and getting to work (8:11, 22). At this time God set the duration of a Levite's career at twenty-five years. Anyone over fifty years of age could continue to help the younger men, but they were "retired" from the more strenuous work (8:23–26). Israel now had an instructed, capable group of ministers. The nation was thereby ready for serious, sustained worship based on the divine principles revealed in Exodus 19–Numbers 8.

By the start of chapter 9 a full year had passed since the Exodus. Thus, God commanded and inspired Israel to keep the Passover and follow His guidance for the future. The observance of the Passover (9:1–5) reminded the people that God's deliverance from Egypt had meaning in the desert as well. The God who created the earth had power to save in any geographical location.

This passage also demonstrates that God accommodated all serious worshippers, whether Jew or Gentile. Numbers 9:6–13 states that a second Passover could be celebrated by anyone becoming unclean just before the observance. Numbers 9:14 adds that aliens who believed in God and wished to participate could as well, as long as they were willing to live by the same rules as the holy people. Clearly, God intended that faith take precedence over racial separation and legalism. The Creator of all peoples desired worship by all people. Those who read the Old Testament as saying God loved only the Jews need to read more closely. Gentile conversion is mentioned in the Old Testament. Caleb, Rahab, Ruth, Hagar, Naaman, Jonah's Ninevites, and others came to faith through God's grace.

God guided Israel's movements in two ways, one miraculous and one quite human. First, God provided a cloud that Israel was to follow (9:15–23). Second, Aaron and the priests blew trumpets when it was time to break camp (10:1–7). The cloud reminded the people that God was ever-present to lead, guide, and inspire worship and confidence. This presence meant that God loved them and reached out in friendship to them. Israel needed to realize their dependence on the Lord for their every movement. Aaron's trumpet blasts were to bring these truths to remembrance (10:8–10).

Now Israel appeared quite capable of moving on to achieve the conquest of the Promised

"Then Peter began to speak: 'I now realize how true it is that God does not show favoritism but accepts men from every nation who fear him and do what is right'" (Acts 10:34–35).

A miracle is an act done by God that bypasses the normal course of nature. God made the regularities in nature that we call natural laws. He is, therefore, not bound by these regularities but can work within nature as He pleases.

Land. They were organized. They had civil and religious leadership. God was with them, which was their most vital asset. Only *they* could stop their march to glory. Sadly, this is just what happened.

■ *This section chronicles some pivotal events*
■ *in the birth of Israel. They have left Egypt,*
■ *accepted a covenant, and rested near Sinai.*
■ *Now they prepared to move on to conquer*
■ *Canaan. They took a census, organized an*
■ *army, organized their priests, purified their*
■ *camp, dedicated certain people and offerings,*
■ *and celebrated their first Passover since leav-*
■ *ing Egypt. Israel's next stop should have been*
■ *Canaan, but instead they began a period of*
■ *wandering in the wilderness for forty years.*

QUESTIONS TO GUIDE YOUR STUDY

1. What was significant about the way Israel arranged their camp and the formation used when they marched?
2. Who were the Nazirites?
3. Who were the Levites?
4. What were the methods God used to guide Israel?

God is always faithful—even when we are not. At times we doubt, complain, cause divisions, or simply lose touch with the Lord. There are always consequences to such behavior, though even these consequences are, thankfully, subject to God's grace. Israel discovered how severe unbelief fed by general discontent can be. They forfeited the immediate opportunity to enter the Promised Land. Still, God fed, clothed, and cared for them. Again, God is always faithful—even when we are not.

THE GOD WHO CORRECTS CHRONIC COMPLAINERS (NUM. 10:11–12:16)

No hint of discontent marred Israel's leaving Sinai. The people arranged themselves and left as they were told (10:11–28). Moses reached out to his non-Jewish brother-in-law and convinced him to be part of God's people (10:29–32). Israel's obedience helped people come to the Lord. God's cloud led them (10:33–34), and their travel became an opportunity for praise and worship (10:35–36). Surely they were meant to act this way always. Surely we are to approach daily life with the intent to follow God's leading, obey God's Word, give witness to God's worth, and praise God for every aspect of life. In this way we can fully integrate faith with family and work.

Despite their initial cheerful obedience, the people soon complained. They got weary of manna, and wailed for the wonderful days in slavery when they had better food (11:1–9). Moses

Israel complained in a similar manner about water in Exodus 17:1–7. Their complaints amounted to testing God. They were ungrateful for the provisions that sustained their lives. In spite of their attitudes, God remained faithful to them.

complained to God about the people's childish complaints (11:10–15). When God called elders to relieve Moses' leadership burden, Joshua (Moses' aide) complained about Moses' lost status (11:16–28). Miriam and Aaron complained that Moses had too much authority, and they complained about his taking an Ethiopian wife (12:1–2). Everyone seemed out of sorts with everyone else. Complaints had caused divisions that were hard to heal.

God responded by continuing to call persons for specific tasks and by correcting misguided beliefs. God answered Israel's dietary wishes by sending quail, then a plague, on all who rejected the Lord's gracious provision (11:18–20; 11:31–34). The Lord's ability to produce such a quantity of meat silenced Moses' doubts (11:21–23). A humble statement from Moses satisfied Joshua's concerns (11:28–30). Miriam and Aaron learned that their own special standing did not entitle them to criticize and rebel against Moses, the one called to lead Israel and to receive divine revelation (11:4–8). God struck Miriam with leprosy, only healing her at Moses' request (12:10–16). Everyone learned that God had provided for them adequately and that it was their job to accept His will for their lives.

Complaining rarely does any good when it arises out of envy, ingratitude, or ambition. Such griping usually leads to bitterness, division, loss of friendship, and an impoverished walk with the Lord. Israel needed to trust God more than ever now, for big decisions were ahead. No one can afford to waste time on petty whining. Most of us have done so, always to our detriment.

THE HIGH COST OF UNBELIEF
(NUM. 13–14)

It is not clear whether Israel's attitude was ever cleansed of doubts about God's goodness and Moses' competence to lead. These two chapters certainly indicate that they continued in their suspicions, for here Israel failed to believe God, do his will, and receive the Promised Land. Unbelief cost them a treasured blessing and consigned them to decades of misery in a harsh desert.

God never changes, so His character and power are always intact. We may face new situations, but He is constantly capable of meeting the needs we have as we serve Him.

At first nothing went wrong. Moses chose and dispatched twelve leaders, one from each tribe, to scope out the Promised Land (13:1–16). He charged them with assessing the land's fruitfulness, population, and defenses (13:17–20). They fulfilled their task, bringing evidence of the land's bounty (13:21–25). Everything seemed in place for a positive report.

Once the report was given, however, difficulties began to surface. Ten of Israel's spies did not interpret the accuracy of God's description of the land (see Exod. 3:7–10), God's deliverance from slavery through the Exodus, God's revelation at Sinai, or God's provision and guidance in the desert to mean that the Lord could also give them the Promised Land. They did not believe that the God who directed their past would direct their future. In this new situation, they saw only fortified cities and fierce foes (13:26–29). Therefore, all the spies but Joshua and Caleb (13:30; 14:6) told the people that victory was impossible (13:31). They even spread ridiculous rumors—such as the land devoured people, and that giants roamed about (13:32–33). They were not the last committee to spread falsehoods to support their position!

From time to time sermons are preached on 13:33—"We seemed like grasshoppers in our own eyes, and we looked the same to them." Often these messages focus on the need for self-esteem. Of course, self-esteem is not an invalid subject. But the point of this text is that Israel did not think enough of God, not that they did not think highly enough of themselves. They were not a great people; they were loved and chosen by a great God who did great things for them and thereby led them to marvelous achievements. In fact, the people thought too highly of themselves here, since they believed they knew better than to do what the Lord had told them to do. Grace and guidance should not be trampled upon in this manner.

The word *remnant* is often used in Scripture to distinguish between the faithful and the unfaithful. Israel always consisted of two groups: those who trusted the Lord and those who went their own way.

Upon hearing the message, the people were grieved (14:1–4). They trusted the majority report rather than their theological heritage. Once again they wished they were back in slavery (14:3; see 11:4–5). This time they even decided to choose new leaders and go back to Egypt (14:4). One last time Moses, Aaron, Caleb, and Joshua asked the people to embrace the land promised (14:7). They urged them to accept God's leadership (14:8), obey God (14:9), and choose faith over fear (14:9). Instead, Israel threatened to stone them (14:10). Faith and obedience were totally absent. Only a small faithful remnant was left.

God settled the dispute decisively (14:10–35). The Lord declared that Israel's problem was, quite simply, a lack of faith. Their problem was contempt for their God despite His many great acts on their behalf (14:10–12). Because of their unbelief, God offered Moses the chance to be the father of a new nation. God would destroy all the unbelievers (14:12; see Exod. 32:9–10).

Moses declined, then prayed for the people (14:13–16; see Exod. 32:11–14). He based his intercessory prayer on God's patience, love, forgiveness, and justice (14:17–19). He made certain that God's name was not impugned (14:15–16).

Moses' prayer was answered, but God did not let Israel go unpunished (14:20–35). God decided to start over with the next generation of Israelites. All the disobedient adults eventually died in the desert, victims of their own unbelief, which was itself fed by complaining. Israel had known the Lord only as a friend to this point, but now they would experience Him as an enemy (14:34). Only Joshua and Caleb were promised a trip to Canaan.

Intercession is not simply about our getting what we want. Its more important function is to have God's will done and God's reputation magnified.

The ten unbelieving spies were the first to die (14:34–38), while Joshua and Caleb lived (14:38). Belatedly and against Moses' advice, the sorrowing people decided to go to war (14:39–43). Of course, they were routed (14:44–45). Without the Lord's help they really did not have any chance for victory.

Unbelief must be avoided at all costs. Faith is the means God uses for salvation. It is also how a believer lives for the Lord after conversion. Like Israel, we must remember God's great acts throughout ancient history right down to our own personal history. The God who parted the Red Sea stands ready to deliver, heal, guide, and inspire today. Unbelief always comes at a high cost. The only question is how high that price will be. The cost was certainly great enough for the desert-bound Israelites.

"For every living soul belongs to me, the father as well as the son—both alike belong to me. The soul who sins is the one who will die" (Ezek. 18:4).

THE GOD WHO PUNISHES AND RENEWS (NUM. 15:1–20:21)

Punishment of the first generation had begun, but God had hardly given up on the chosen people. The second generation must be prepared to conquer Canaan. Over the next thirty-eight years the Lord and Moses conducted this training. Unbelief is not genetic, so God could begin afresh with another group.

One way God demonstrated His ongoing relationship with Israel was through the giving of new laws. Four sets of laws appear in chapter 15. First, the Lord commanded that the first sacrifices made in the land were to be accompanied by grain and drink offerings (15:1–20). Adding this extra amount would remind them throughout their history what a great blessing the land was to them (15:21). It is important to note that non-Israelites were included in these laws (15:13–16). Once again the Lord was careful to include all persons of faith in worship.

Once again God distinguishes between true faith and legalism. Bringing sacrifices only atones for sin when the proper attitude accompanies the required offering. Unrepentant persons cannot be forgiven.

Second, God declared the difference between unintentional and intentional sins (15:22–31). Simply put, a sinner may as well not bring a sacrifice if it is not brought in repentance and humility (15:30–31). Those who despised God by breaking His laws and then taking forgiveness for granted received nothing from God but judgment.

Third, God told Israel to execute a blatant Sabbath breaker (15:32–36). Fourth, the Lord approved of tassels on garments, perhaps because such clothing reminded them of His many gracious standards (15:37–41). This law is like Deuteronomy 6:4–9, where God told Israel to make every effort to remember and live by the Word of God. Each of these laws demonstrated that the Lord still planned to give Israel the land. The question is whether the people would obey Him and receive their inheritance.

Remarkably, Israel continued to rebel against God even after the Lord's wrath in Numbers 14 and renewed promises in Numbers 15. A coalition of Levites and community leaders opposed Moses and Aaron (16:1–3). Their goal was to gain the high priest's position for Korah, who was not one of Aaron's sons. Apparently, the Korah faction viewed the high priest's role more as one of status and power rather than as a theological ministry dedicated to holiness and instruction. God removed the rebels in miraculous fashion (16:4–40), which resulted in the community accusing Moses of killing God's people (16:41). In response, God sent a plague that killed the insolent rebels (16:42–50).

Chapters 17–19 reinforce God's chosen leaders. First, 17:1–13 dramatically emphasized Aaron's call to be high priest. Leaders from Israel were told to present a staff to be laid alongside Aaron's (17:1–7). When they returned the next day, Aaron's staff had budded and produced almonds (17:8–9). In this way the people were shown Aaron's primacy (17:10–12), which in turn led to a healthy fear of the Lord (17:13).

Second, 18:1–32 restates the duties of the priests and Levites. No other group had God's approval. These laws made the priests responsible for offenses against the sanctuary (18:1). They were to recruit sufficient helpers (18:2–4), care for the sanctuary (18:5–7), and handle all the sacrifices (18:8–32). They were to accept gladly the best part of the sacrifices, and were to be satisfied with having no set tribal inheritance (18:21–32). With controversy in the air, God

"I am not saying this because I am in need, for I have learned to be content whatever the circumstances. I know what it is to be in need, and I know what it is to have plenty. I have learned the secret of being content in any and every situation, whether well fed or hungry, whether living in plenty or in want. I can do everything through him who gives me strength" (Phil. 4:11–13).

saw fit to instruct the worship leaders on how to avoid corruption. Simply put, they were to serve the Lord by serving the people, making worship what God intended, and being satisfied with the material wealth (or lack thereof) that came with their vocation.

Third, 19:1–22 emphasizes the value of ritual cleansing, which reminded Israel how pervasive sin was in their midst. A special ritual is introduced here to effect cleansing that involved the using of a red heifer as a burnt offering. Once consumed, the animal's ashes were kept for use in cleansing ceremonies (19:1–10). As was explained in Leviticus 11–15, touching dead bodies caused Israelites to become unclean. Therefore, 19:11–22 explains how those who handled dead bodies could be cleansed. Apparently the ashes mentioned in 19:1–10 were used in the ritual.

Just as chapter 17 emphasized Israel's need to honor God's chosen priest and chapter 18 emphasized the priests' need to take their work with utmost seriousness, so chapter 19 keeps the need for cleanness before the people. If all parties took these admonitions seriously, then incidents like the Korah rebellion would be much less likely in the future.

It is sad that the Lord has to punish anyone, much less a great spiritual leader. Numbers 20:1–21 describes God disciplining Moses. This makes it one of the most tragic passages in the Bible. Not even the best Christians are sinless, and they must suffer for their transgressions. Still, when faced with the consequences of their actions, great believers turn to the Lord. They find ways to be faithful in the new circumstances. Moses illustrates all these principles in this sad but inspiring account.

After announcing Miriam's death (20:1), the text relates a familiar situation. Israel needed water, wished they were dead, hated the desert, and so forth (20:2–5). As always, Moses and Aaron received specific directions from the Lord on how to solve the problem. They were to speak to a rock, from which would flow the necessary water (20:6–8).

No Christian, no matter how influential, can take credit for God's work without suffering the consequences of such arrogance. A lack of faith will lead to many sins, including seeking God's glory for ourselves.

Instead, Moses did two things he had never done. First, he did not give credit to God. Rather, he asked if he and Aaron had to bring water from the rock (20:9–10). Second, he struck the rock; he did not speak to it (20:11). Water flowed from the rock, but the miracle's success was not the only concern. Moses failed to honor God by obeying Him. He also failed to glorify God in the people's sight by not attributing all miraculous power to the Lord. God declared that Moses did not believe in Him sufficiently to "honor" Him as holy in this instance (20:12).

God punished Moses by denying him the blessing of leading Israel to conquer the Promised Land (20:12). He had to lead the people forward, and he did so in 20:14–21. But his own hopes had been dashed. What did he do? Did he rebel like other Israelites? Did he become a chronic complainer like so many? He did not. Moses led, instructed, and prepared the next generation without hope of sharing their success. His greatness included enough commitment to God to serve Him under less-than-appealing circumstances. A lack of faith cost him the chance to enjoy Canaan, but renewed faith helped him complete his divinely assigned leadership task.

Clearly, sin costs nonbelievers and believers alike. Of course, the price is higher for nonbelievers. So Christians should do all that is necessary to nurture faith in themselves and others. Unbelief is a dread enemy that offers only pain and defeat. Faith, on the other hand, bestows the gifts of character, peace, and wise living.

This section also demonstrates God's willingness to forgive and renew. Both Moses and Israel's first generation were not cast off. God sustained them. God kept feeding and guiding them. Thus, Israel discovered that the Lord is merciful to the broken (see Exod. 34:6–7). Failure is not the final word when God is so gracious.

- *These chapters record one disaster and*
- *missed opportunity after another. A whole*
- *generation of Israelites died in the desert for*
- *their disobedience. Even Moses lost the*
- *privilege of entering Canaan.*

QUESTIONS TO GUIDE YOUR STUDY

1. What were some of the things Israel complained about?
2. What were the consequences of Israel's refusal to move on and possess Canaan?
3. What prompted Korah's rebellion, and what were the consequences?
4. What did Moses do to displease God?

PART THREE
THE GOD WHO RENEWS:
NUMBERS 20:22–36:13

There were now two Israels coexisting in the desert. One was the older generation that had to die, never possessing the Promised Land because of their unbelief. The other was the second generation that was growing, maturing, and preparing to possess Canaan. God provided manna, water, and an experienced leader for both. He also protected the people from military defeat and dangerous spiritual sins. God remained faithful to His people. More specifically, God's character ensured that He would keep promises made to Abraham in Genesis 12:1–9. Abraham's descendants would receive the Promised Land as an inheritance. To keep this promise, God sustained, gave victory, offered instruction, and continued to discipline.

"The Lord appeared to Abram and said, 'To your offspring I will give this land.' So he built an altar there to the LORD, who had appeared to him" (Gen. 12:7).

GOD SUSTAINS AND GIVES VICTORY (NUM. 20:22–21:35)

Three accounts demonstrate how God sustained key ingredients of Israelite life. First, upon Aaron's death the Lord sustained the nation's spiritual leadership by providing a smooth transition from Aaron's high priesthood to his son Eleazar (20:22–29). The sanctuary continued to operate, which meant that forgiveness and instruction were available to worshipers. Second, when the people complained, the Lord sent a plague to chastise them (21:4–6). Once again Moses interceded for the people, so the Lord honored his leadership (21:8–9). God kept teaching Israel how to believe and obey through this incident. Third, God guaranteed safety as they journeyed through Moab (21:10–20). Israel remained secure through God's power.

Two accounts also highlight the Lord's ability to give specific victories. First, Israel encountered and defeated the army of "the Canaanite king of Arad" because God gave the people the strength to do so (21:1–3). This victory foreshadowed greater victories to come. When Israel was threatened, God responded. Second, God enabled Israel to defeat the Amorites (21:21–35). Through these victories Israel possessed land. These episodes prove that Israel could have won such victories years ago if they had only trusted the Lord. These conquests also instilled confidence in the people that they would indeed inherit the Promised Land.

GOD PROTECTS HIS WORD (NUM. 22–25)

Israel now began the third stage of their journey. After the Exodus they spent time at Mount Sinai (Exod. 19:1–Num. 10:12) and in the desert (Num. 10:12–22:1). Now they camped "across from Jericho" (22:1) and in the plains of Moab. Here they stayed until they began the conquest of Canaan. As they came closer to their goals, their opponents understandably tried to stop them. In particular they attempted to destroy Israel's relationship with God before further battles could be fought. To do so they tried to hire a prophet of questionable character and then lured them into pagan worship rites. Neither ploy worked, for God protected Israel by protecting His word. The accuracy of God's Word and the enduring quality of God's promises guaranteed that these plots were doomed to failure.

The Balaam accounts in Numbers 22–24 are well known. Moab and Midian feared Israel, so Balak, king of Moab, hoped to hire Balaam to curse Israel (22:1–6). Balaam declined once due to God's orders (22:7–14), then agreed when the Lord granted permission (22:15–20). Balak hoped that Balaam could manipulate God, perhaps by magic. Balaam was not a magician, but his willingness to explore the possibility of cursing Israel for money is troubling.

Perhaps God wanted Balaam to exercise wisdom and not go to Balak, or maybe some unspecified event angered God before Balaam left. At any rate, God's anger flared. While riding along, Balaam's donkey saw the angel of God ready to kill them, and she lay down. When Balaam beat her, the animal spoke a word of warning (22:21–34). God was not interested in money or sacrifice. Rather, Balaam was to say only what God ordered (22:35–41). Apparently, God knew that Balaam was not as used to speaking only God's words as was Moses!

Once in Balak's presence, Balaam spoke four times about Israel. Never did he curse them. The first message emphasized Israel's election by God (23:7–8), holiness (23:9), numerical strength (23:10), and overall blessedness (23:10). In other words, he did not do exactly what Barak hired him to do. When Balak complained, Balaam replied that he had simply spoken God's words (23:11–12).

Balak tried again. He hoped that moving to a new spot might help Balaam curse Israel (23:13–14). Like many ancient people, he probably believed that the Lord's power was confined to specific places. Or, he may have thought God would change His mind. Either

"They have left the straight way and wandered off to follow the way of Balaam son of Beor, who loved the wages of wickedness. But he was rebuked for his wrongdoing by a donkey—a beast without speech—who spoke with a man's voice and restrained the prophet's madness" (2 Pet. 2:15–16).

way he soon discovered that God does not misspeak or change His mind (23:18–19). God's promises to Abraham must come true (23:7–10), and God's work through Moses will not be in vain (23:18–24). God cannot be manipulated. God is not limited by geographical setting. God's Word cannot fail.

Angry and defiant, Balak tried one last time. To his dismay, Balaam blessed all Israel (24:3–5), predicted they would eventually have a great king and kingdom (24:6–7), and linked their power to God's work on their behalf (24:8–9). Finally, Balaam predicted that Israel would defeat all their foes (24:15–24). God's Word is perfect even when delivered by a prophet for hire like Balaam. Gratefully, the power of God's Word transcends the speaker's weaknesses. God protects and blesses His Word no matter who delivers it. This principle in part explains how good things sometimes result from a flawed ministry.

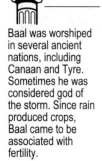

Baal was worshiped in several ancient nations, including Canaan and Tyre. Sometimes he was considered god of the storm. Since rain produced crops, Baal came to be associated with fertility.

Balak now realized that Israel could only be stopped if they stopped worshiping the Lord. Therefore, Moabite women invited Israelite men to worship Baal with them (25:1–8). Baal was a fertility god who was thought to make farmers prosperous, kings strong, and women fertile. To worship him a person had to offer sacrifices, eat special festival meals, and engage in sexual acts. Often, male and female prostitutes were provided for Baal's devoted followers. God judged the people for their actions (25:4), and only drastic measures stopped God's punishing plague (25:6–9). God took their idolatry and adultery seriously. He blessed the man who stopped the immorality and cautioned the people to never act that way again (25:10–18). Sadly, Israel's later history was filled with Baal worship. Elijah (see 1 Kings 18:1–46) and others fought bravely against this sin, but they were often in the minority. Worshiping sex, money, and power remains popular in many places even today.

Numbers 22–25 demonstrates that Israel's future depended on commitment to God and the Word of God. The Lord knows and declares this principle and protects His Word scrupulously. In this way God renewed and instructed the people. For their part, Israel faltered at times, but truly committed believers rose to the challenge of faith. These faithful ones enjoyed all the certain blessings of obedience.

The second generation served the Lord effectively (see Judg. 2:7). They also conquered the Promised Land. No subsequent generation ever accomplished more under such difficult circumstances.

GOD PREPARES ISRAEL FOR VICTORY (NUM. 26:1–36:13)

In this final portion of Numbers, the Lord takes pains to ready Israel for victory. For this second generation of Israelites, victory can only be defined as possession of Canaan. These chapters consist of a census (26:1–65), worship-related commands (chaps. 27–30), and orders about dividing the land (chaps. 31–36). Each part of this section expresses growing confidence that this generation will heed God's Word and enter the Promised Land.

IDENTIFYING ISRAEL'S ARMY (26:1–65)

Preparation for conquest required that Israel's fighting force be identified. The census here had the same purpose as the census in Numbers 1, which was to count Israel's potential army. Thirty-eight years have passed between censuses, and only Joshua, Caleb, and Moses remained from the first counting (26:63–65). The number of fighters declined by a mere 1,820 men, so God sustained significant numbers of Israelites in the desert.

This episode proves once again that Israel's law was not oblivious to women's needs. These sisters were allowed the same rights as men in this instance.

A prayer of Moses the man of God.

"Lord, you have been our dwelling place throughout all generations. Before the mountains were born or you brought forth the earth and the world, from everlasting to everlasting you are God" (Ps. 90:1–2).

CONFIRMING ISRAEL'S HOLINESS (NUM. 27–30)

Five sisters approached Moses with an inheritance question. Supremely confident that God would give Israel the land, they asked if they could inherit their father's land since they had no brothers. They feared the loss of family property (27:1–4). God ruled that daughters could indeed inherit land, and that land should stay in a clan's possession if at all possible (27:5–11). This discussion was evidence of the women's faith in the Lord. They humbly sought the Lord based on the certainty that God's promises would come true. God rewarded that faith just as He rewarded the faithful throughout the Bible. Though rewards vary, the Lord's promises and faithful character never do.

Moses had known for some time that he would not lead the conquest of Canaan, but his successor had not been revealed. In response to Moses' prayer on the matter, God chose Joshua (27:12–17). A veteran of the Exodus and wilderness era, Joshua possessed experience, faith, and God's Spirit (27:18). He received Moses' authority in the presence of Eleazar, the high priest, and all Israel (27:19–23). This transfer of leadership, like the one from Aaron to Eleazar in Numbers 20:22–29, reflected God's continuing commitment to the chosen people. Like God's Word, God's commitments never flag or fail. They transcend time, circumstances, and human failure. God's character is eternally stable. Joshua became a crucial human instrument as God kept His Word to Israel.

Just as the last generation received commands concerning purity and worship after their census (see Num. 5:1–10:10), so the second generation now heard instruction concerning offerings, festivals, and vows (28:1–30:16) after theirs. This new generation must learn what their parents never did: they can only succeed through proper obedience which included bringing sacrifices on normal days (28:1–8). It also meant offering them on the Sabbath (28:9–10), the first of the month (28:11–15), and on special days like Passover (28:16–25) and First Fruits (28:26–31). Israel needed God's forgiveness. Since they sinned regularly, they needed regular sacrifices. If they left sin unchecked, then they could not expect a holy God to honor them.

Of course, no sacrifice was more important than those associated with the day of Atonement (see Lev. 16). Therefore, Israel received specific instructions about what offerings were required on the first day of the seventh month (29:1–6), the tenth day (29:7–11), and each day associated with the day of Atonement itself (29:12–40). Again, atonement for sins was vital to their salvation just as it is to ours. They could not afford to neglect God's revealed means for cleansing from sin.

God intended for Israel to take its commitments seriously. Thus, chapter 30 explains the importance of keeping vows made to the Lord. Of course, Leviticus 27 addressed the same subject, but it served as a call to decision for the first generation. Here Moses bound men and women to their vows (30:1–2), though a husband or father could annul a rash vow (30:3–16). God was not interested in trapping people into a commitment or in making them keep a rash vow made in a fit of panic. At the same time, promises made in good faith were to be kept. Israel's word was supposed to be their bond. In this way they confirmed their status as holy people, as a

"Again, you have heard that it was said to the people long ago, 'Do not break your oath, but keep the oaths you have made to the Lord.' But I tell you, Do not swear at all: either by heaven, for it is God's throne; or by the earth, for it is his footstool; or by Jerusalem, for it is the city of the Great King. And do not swear by your head, for you cannot make even one hair white or black. Simply let your 'Yes' be 'Yes,' and your 'No,' 'No'; anything beyond this comes from the evil one" (Matt. 5:33–37).

"Holy wars" were called only by God and were not repeated. Thus, it is inappropriate to apply many principles for today from the battles Israel fought in the desert. These were unique instances that served as God's judgment against Canaan (see Gen. 15:13–16). God did not make these wars ongoing obligations.

nation determined to be holy as their God was holy (see Lev. 11:44).

FIRST VICTORIES IN THE HOLY LAND (NUM. 31–32)

Though his successor had been named, Moses could not retire. He still had God-ordained work to do. His first task was to lead Israel in battle against the Midianites, the people who instigated the idolatry in Numbers 25. Moses mustered a thousand soldiers from each tribe and Israel won a complete victory (31:1–12). Contrary to orders, however, they kept some spoil (31:12). Moses then had them execute the majority of the people, presumably because of their role in leading Israel astray, though the text does not say specifically (31:13–20). Afterwards, the people divided the spoil (31:21–47). Some was kept for offerings to the Lord (31:48–54).

As with the victory recounted in 21:1–5, this triumph demonstrated God's power to make Israel succeed. God could have led the first generation forward if they had only believed. Blessings were given when Israel obeyed, just as Leviticus 26 promised.

Moses' second task was to begin the process of dividing the land among the people. The tribes of Gad and Reuben, as well as half the tribe of Manasseh, requested that they receive their land on the east side of the Jordan River (32:1–5). They asked this for business reasons, but Moses feared another rejection of the Promised Land similar to the one in Numbers 13–14 (32:6–15). Moses averted this threat by securing the promise of these tribes to help their kinsmen conquer Canaan before possessing their inheritance (32:16–42). These tribes agreed to the proposal, which once again demonstrated the people's conviction that God would give them the land. It also proved their devotion to one another.

Israel understood now that commitment to the Lord was the key to their future. They saw God give them victory in battle. They followed Moses' instructions. They learned from their parents' mistakes, and they learned from their own. They were becoming mature believers.

PREPARATION FOR OCCUPATION (NUM. 33–36)

As Israel prepared for war, Moses led them to make specific preparations. To remind them of how God had guided and provided, Moses wrote down the places where they had journeyed (33:1–49). He did so as a prelude to dividing the Promised Land. For Israel, history meant knowing why the past unfolded as it did so that the present and future could be understood properly. Each stop along the way proved God's grace, faithfulness, power, and love. Based on God's great acts on their behalf, Moses commanded them to possess Canaan (33:50–56). They needed to create their own (positive) history, and the book of Joshua proves they did just that.

The casting of lots in this situation was done because it did not matter where each tribe would go. Moses simply attempted to be fair to all concerned.

Next, Moses set the boundaries for the Promised Land (34:1–12) and determined that the tribal territories would be assigned by casting lots (34:13–15). This procedure kept the people from vying for the best portions of the land. Civil war was thereby avoided. The casting of lots also emphasized to the people that the whole land was God's gift. All of it was given by God's grace, and it was to be received with gratitude. Moses also appointed tribal leaders who were to assign each family a place within their tribal land (34:16–29). Eleazar the high priest, Joshua, and Caleb are the most recognizable names. These individuals continued to serve God by serving God's people. They provided wisdom, continuity, experience, and spiritual insight for Israel.

Then Moses set aside cities and pastures for the Levites, since they were not given a specific tribal area of their own (35:1–5). Six towns were designated "cities of refuge," places where those who killed someone accidentally could flee for safety from avenging relatives of the deceased (35:6–34). In ancient cultures, the avenger of blood was a sort of "policeman" who made sure that justice was done. Of course, in many instances the avenger could fail to get all the facts. Thus, a person claiming innocence could flee to a city of refuge. Avengers of blood could seek justice from the city elders, so the system did not simply protect criminals. Clearly, God's concern was for mercy for the innocent, punishment for the wicked, and justice for all concerned.

Finally, Moses heard from Zelophehad's daughters (see chap. 27) again (36:1–13). This time clan leaders secured a ruling that the women marry within their tribe so that Manasseh's share in the Promised Land would not diminish. Land had become precious to them, for it was God's gift. It had to be protected against negligence or even the lack of males in a specific family. Their God-given inheritance had to be possessed, protected, and treasured. Raised in the desert, this generation knew how important the physical blessing of land could be. They also grasped that faithfulness to God was the means by which their hopes would be realized.

CONCLUSION

Numbers holds a bittersweet place in the Bible. On the one hand, there is hope in Numbers 1:1–10:10 and victory in Numbers 21–36. God kept all His promises to Israel, and continued to emphasize that faith and obedience would result in blessing. God's faithfulness and Israel's well being are not in question.

On the other hand, episodes in Numbers 13–20 generate several negative comments in the rest of the Bible. Israel's first generation is remembered for squandering opportunities, rebellion, and unbelief. From Deuteronomy to Numbers, accounts in Numbers illustrate comments about greed, faithlessness, and idolatry. Therefore, Numbers 13–20 ought to be read as a sober warning to all persons of faith.

"Now the just shall live by faith: but if any man draw back, my soul shall have no pleasure in him. But we are not of them who draw back unto perdition; but of them that believe to the saving of the soul" (Heb. 10:38–39, KJV).

Still, when Numbers closes, hope springs anew. A new generation is hungry for the Lord and the fulfillment of His promises. A second high priest and Moses' replacement stand ready to serve. God's grace has overcome all obstacles and continues to do so in Israel's history right through the crucifixion and resurrection of Jesus Christ.

■ *Slowly, painfully, the old generation began*
■ *to die. God remained faithful to them, pro-*
■ *viding food, clothing, guidance, and even*
■ *some military victories. God instructed*
■ *Moses to prepare Joshua to be Israel's new*
■ *leader. Moses recounted the sad history of*
■ *Israel's wandering in the wilderness. The last*
■ *few chapters point to a more hopeful*
■ *future---a time when Israel can expect to*
■ *approach Canaan once again.*

QUESTIONS TO GUIDE YOUR STUDY

1. What did Balak repeatedly try to get Balaam to do? How did Balaam respond?
2. What was the purpose of the two censuses (chap. 1 and chap. 26)?
3. Who was Moses' successor, and how was he chosen?
4. Who were Zelophedad's daughters, and what did they ask of Moses?

The following is a collection of Broadman & Holman published reference sources used for this work. They are provided here to accompany the reader's need for more specific information or for an expanded treatment of the books of Levitucs and Numbers. All of these works will greatly aid the reader's study, teaching, and presentation of the Bible's prophetic books.

Cate, Robert L. *An Introduction to the Old Testament and Its Study*. An introductory work presenting background information, issues related to interpretation, and summaries of each book of the Old Testament.

Dockery, David S., Kenneth A. Mathews, and Robert B. Sloan. *Foundations for Biblical Interpretation: A Complete Library of Tools and Resources*. A comprehensive introduction to matters relating to the composition and interpretation of the entire Bible. This work includes a discussion of the geographical, historical, cultural, religious, and political backgrounds of the Bible.

Farris, T. V. *Mighty to Save: A Study in Old Testament Soteriology*. A wonderful evaluation of many Old Testament passages that teach about salvation. This work makes a conscious attempt to apply Old Testament teachings to the Christian life.

Francisco, Clyde T. *Introducing the Old Testament*. Revised edition. An introductory guide to each of the books of the Old Testament. This work includes a discussion on how to interpret the Old Testament.

Holman Bible Dictionary. An exhaustive, alphabetically arranged resource of Bible-related subjects. An excellent tool of definitions and other information on people, places, things, and events mentioned in the Bible or forming the historical context of the Bible.

Holman Bible Handbook. A summary treatment of each book of the Bible that offers outlines, commentary on key themes and sections, illustrations, charts, maps, and full-color photos. This tool also provides an accent on broader theological teachings of the Bible.

Holman Book of Biblical Charts, Maps and Reconstructions. This easy-to-use work provides numerous events and drawings of objects, buildings, and cities mentioned in the Bible.

Honeycutt, Roy Lee, Jr. *Leviticus, Numbers, Deuteronomy.* (Layman's Bible Book Commentary, vol. 3). A popular-level treatment of the books of Leviticus, Numbers, and Deuteronomy. This easy-to-use volume provides a relevant and practical perspective for the reader.

Sandy, D. Brent and Ronald L. Giese Jr. *Cracking Old Testament Codes: A Guide to Interpreting the Literary Genres of the Old Testament.* This book is designed to make scholarly discussions available to preachers and teachers.

Smith, Gary V. *The Prophets as Preachers: An Introduction to the Hebrew Prophets.* An examination of the impact of the prophets and their writings on contemporary Christians. This book is an excellent college or seminary level textbook and a comprehensive resource for pastors and other serious Bible students.

Smith, Ralph L. *Old Testament Theology: Its History, Method and Message.* A comprehensive treatment of various issues relating to Old Testament theology. This work was written for university and seminary students, ministers, and advanced lay teachers.